A TASTE
FOR ALL SEASONS

A TASTE
FOR
ALL SEASONS

A Celebration of American Food

The Chefs of ARA Fine Dining
in association with David Paul Larousse

THE HARVARD COMMON PRESS
Harvard and Boston, Massachusetts

The Harvard Common Press
535 Albany Street
Boston, Massachusetts

Printed in the United States of America

Library of Congress Cataloging-in-Publication Data
A taste for all seasons : a celebration of American food / by the chefs from ARA fine dining in association with David Paul Larousse.
   p. cm.
   ISBN 1-55832-020-2 : $24.95
   1. Cookery. I. Larousse, David Paul, 1949– . II. ARA Services.
TX714.T36 1990
641.5—dc20
                                                     89-24688
                                                       CIP

Food styling by William Della Ventura
Color photographs by Dean Della Ventura
Drawings by David Paul Larousse
Cover design by Joyce C. Weston
Text design by Linda Ziedrich

10 9 8 7 6 5 4 3 2 1

CONTENTS

LIST OF
COLOR ILLUSTRATIONS

FOREWORD

Of all the comments we receive from patrons of the restaurants in our Fine Dining Division—the Carnelian Room, in San Francisco; Atwater's, in Portland, Oregon; The 95th, in Chicago; and The Tower, in Philadelphia—the most frequent are requests for recipes; second to these are inquiries about where to purchase the ingredients with which our chefs create their dishes.

Writing a cookbook is probably a secret wish of many chefs, but it is hardly an easy dream to realize. Nevertheless, spurred by the continuous interest of our patrons, we eventually decided to work toward creating a collection of recipes. This not only would respond to the many requests for recipes and introduce some of the specialty food producers who supply food products native to North America, it also would give our chefs an opportunity to fulfill their secret literary desires.

ARA Services began thirty years ago with the merger of two small vending companies—the Davidson Brothers of California and the Automatic Merchandising Company of Chicago. From the beginning, the company's business was service management; its one thousand employees provided vended food and refreshment services in nineteen states. Today, ARA is one of the world's largest diversified services companies, employing more than one hundred and twenty thousand employees in all fifty states and five foreign countries to meet the various needs of ten million people daily.

ARA is made up of twenty divisions within four service areas, which provide services as diverse as refreshments at ballpark stadiums and recreational facilities in our national park system to "meals on wheels" and health-care nutrition for senior citizens. Though the Fine Dining Division is small in relation to the whole organization, the company has a long-standing tradition of commitment to the chefs at these dining operations. Its willingness to give creative young chefs the necessary resources, the raw materials, and, most importantly, the freedom to develop their culinary craft fosters an environment where innovation flourishes. It is this commitment that has put these restaurants in the vanguard of contemporary American cuisine.

I joined ARA in 1982 as chef de cuisine at The 95th Restaurant, located atop the John Hancock Center in Chicago. At the time, the restaurant was going through a redesign that included a new menu focusing on innovative cuisine using ingredients unique to the Midwest. The public's response to this new focus was enthusiastic—a clear indication that American appreciation of innovation in the culinary arts had matured considerably.

Twice every year, I meet with the chefs from our fine-dining restaurants to gather new ideas for our menus, which change each season. As a result of these meetings, we began to collect recipes that we felt characterized our cooking style.

Our philosophy of fine dining includes sharing the knowledge we gain about food with our customers through menu notes, staff training, and seminars and related food events. There are many misconceptions about food and cooking: what better place to dispel them than in a dining environment? We agreed that our cookbook should uphold this same philosophy, educating as it entertained.

Many professionals who made significant contributions to this project have since moved on in their careers. Deborah Hartz, now editor-in-chief at *Cook's Magazine,* was instrumental in compiling the initial manuscript. Several recipes included in this cookbook and still featured on several of our menus were developed by former ARA chefs: Billy Della Ventura and myself, previously of The 95th; Pierre Chechi of Penn's Wood Catering, in Philadelphia; David Asher, *tournant* at the Carnelian Room; Bill Geary of Atwater's; and Richard Buthe at Fidelity Bank in Philadelphia. Billy Della Ventura also helped gather material for the book. He worked closely with David Larousse as his literary assistant and was responsible for the food styling.

The majority of the recipes, however, were developed by four of our current chefs—Gabriel Elicetche of the Carnelian Room, who brings a rich tradition of Basque cuisine to his repertoire; George Poston of Atwater's, a graduate of the Culinary Institute of America in Hyde Park, New York; David DiGregorio, a 1980 graduate of Johnson and Wales University, who began as a saucier at The 95th in 1982 and is now chef de cuisine there; and Manfred Bast, a noted master pastry chef from Germany, who is actively involved in the American Culinary Federation and runs the brigade at The Tower in Philadelphia.

This book has been several years in the making, and a great many individuals have contributed to the project. We think the end result does justice to their time and effort. The cuisine of the United States has gone through many phases and is still relatively young by the standards of the melting-pot tradition it represents. But it can now stand on its own. We hope that you find *A Taste for All Seasons* to be persuasive testimony to this new maturity.

CHRISTIAN DE VOS
Vice President, ARA Services, Inc.
Fine Dining Division

ACKNOWLEDGMENTS

We wish to offer our heartfelt thanks to the following individuals for their contributions to *A Taste for All Seasons:*

- Peter L. Pratt, broadcast personality, video producer, gourmand, and bon vivant, for helping us to come up with the book title.
- Robert J. Palumbo of ARA Services, Inc., for giving the go ahead for this project.
- Charlie Gillespie, Dick Vent, and John Farquharson of ARA Services, Inc., for the support they have given our chefs, which made this book possible.
- William Della Ventura, for the first round of recipe testing and for the exceptionally fine food styling for the color photography.
- Randall Goodman and Kamel Jabari, sommeliers at the Carnelian Room, for the wine suggestions.
- John B. Foley, president of The Connecticut Brewing Company, for historical and technical information on beer and beer brewing.
- Bruce Meyer, proprietor of Geary's of Beverly Hills, for lending the silverware, china, and accessories used in the color photography.
- The cheese, wine, beer, brandy, caviar, fish, chocolate, jam, jelly, and vinegar producers and the produce growers and small farmers who extended friendly greetings, background information on their products, and lots of tasting samples.
- David K. O'Neil, General Manager of the Reading Terminal Market, Philadelphia, for background material on the Reading Terminal Market.
- The recipe testers: Jeannette Dideriksen, Lisa Giel, Wong Keng, Richard Marquardt, Scott Rishel, Marilyn Stanton, Randy Sterrett, Darla Swanson, David Glazer, Charles Boswell, Carlton Winkfield, William Mayer, Ercu Ecrument, Jeffrey Thomas, and Linda Hawbaker.

INTRODUCTION

In the December 17, 1972, issue of the *New York Times Sunday Magazine,* there appeared a story profiling a restaurateur from Lyon, France, entitled "A Simple Lunch with Paul Bocuse." On the cover of the magazine was a photograph of the restaurateur at a produce market, with the caption, "Paul Bocuse, one of France's greatest cooks, goes marketing."

At the time, I was in my second year of training at the Culinary Institute of America in Hyde Park, New York. It was years ago, yet I still recall the story in vivid detail. The honesty of Bocuse's manner of cooking and of operating a restaurant touched a chord in my culinary soul.

Bocuse made early morning forays to the farmers' market outside Lyon, where the local growers brought their choicest produce. It was here that he put into practice the axiom his mentor, Ferdinand Point, had taught him: "I'm not hard to please, as long as you give me the best." This constant search for intensely fresh ingredients made sense to me. I imagined the chef in a farmer's field as the sun began to light the early morning sky. I pictured him bantering with the grower as he reached down to grasp a tiny, perfect head of lettuce. I could see him cutting the lettuce at its base, the early morning dew still glistening on its leaves. Then he would rise, turn to the grower, and place his order for the day. It was an enchanting image. I thought, "This is like soul food, only in another country. This is a passion for life, transferred to the kitchen. This is how I must work."

Six months later, I was out of school. My first job as a cook was in a stylish restaurant in a picturesque village on Cape Cod, an establishment I would later describe as a food factory. Six hundred dinners served on a Saturday night was the norm. I worked in that kitchen twelve hours a day, six days a week, for the entire summer season. I learned a good deal, but I couldn't help wondering how any cook with such a schedule could have time to visit the local fishermen. All the raw foodstuffs were ordered by telephone and delivered in two-ton trucks. This was not the way to work with the freshest of the fresh and to express one's passion for living in the culinary craft. I longed for an opportunity to develop personal relationships with the individuals who produced the materials with which I worked.

The following summer, I learned that a restaurateur at the end of Long Island was seeking a working chef. I met with the owner shortly thereafter to discuss the terms of the position. By the end of our meeting, we had come to an agreement. I'll never know whether she could sense the culinary passion bubbling within me or if the fact that it was late spring and the opening weekend of the season was fast approaching was responsible. Either way, ecstatic, I prepared to dive in.

Eastern Long Island has a long agricultural heritage. Long Island potatoes, duck, and some of the finest seafood found in the North Atlantic are perhaps the most distinguished representatives of the bounty available. But there is more. The year-round residents who work their small plots of land during the warmer months sell their vegetables to the summer trade—restaurateurs and visitors, mostly from New York City—to augment their incomes. For me, it was a godsend.

First, I decided to compose my menu daily, based on the availability of ingredients. Instead of using a traditional printed menu, I purchased a half-dozen twelve-by-eight-inch slate boards, on which each day's menu would be hand-lettered. With this spontaneous approach in mind, I then ventured out to meet the local suppliers.

My first contact was a man who raised poultry. Two or three times a week, I would drive out to his small farm, and he would supply me with the freshest chicken and duck I had ever tasted, dressed to order, with head and feet intact.

Another gentleman, a Brooklynite who spent his summers in the area, took me and my sous chef out in his twelve-foot skiff at 5:00 A.M. one brisk spring day. All of that morning out in Long Island Sound, we reeled in bluefish, monkfish, and flounder. We spent the afternoon on the shore, wading into the shallow surf, barefoot, pant legs rolled up, digging for littleneck and cherrystone clams. We brought our catch back to the kitchen and gave our host an open invitation for dinner as our way of thanking him for the hands-on tour. For the rest of the summer, he brought me a splendid supply of fish, day in and day out.

Local produce was just as plentiful, provided by a variety of local growers. One elderly Austrian woman, who grew a dozen or so different crops during the warm months, always invited me into her home for tea whenever I came shopping. Her vine-ripened tomatoes were inconsistent in shape and size but sweet and juicy, bursting with flavor. I also purchased from several other small farmers in the area, making morning trips to their homes and vegetable stands.

My stint at that fifty-seat restaurant in eastern Long Island was glorious, an experience that significantly shaped my growth as a chef. In the years since, I have found myself behind the range in all kinds of operations, large and small, urban and rural, from New England to the West Indies, from Strasbourg, France, to San Francisco, California. In many cases, I developed a network of suppliers over the telephone. More often than not, especially in the city, the demands of production did not permit personal contact with the producers. The close contact that I had enjoyed on Long Island was the exception, not the rule. Thus, it was with considerable enthusiasm that I embarked upon the writing of this book. It became an opportunity to relive the time when I worked closely with the people who made my style of cooking—and the cooking of the chefs represented in these pages—possible.

DAVID PAUL LAROUSSE

GLOSSARY
OF CULINARY TERMS

Although it is impossible to collect everything we know about cooking in a single volume, we want to share as much knowledge and as many techniques as possible. The terms defined here are all used in the four restaurants represented in this book. Familiarizing yourself with them will provide the foundation from which to create the dishes that follow.

AL DENTE: Literally meaning "to the tooth" or "to the bite," this term is used to describe pasta and vegetables cooked until they are tender but not mushy. They should be somewhat firm and resilient when bitten into.

BLANCH: To place food in boiling salted water, stock, or other liquid, in order to cook it partially, set its color, or facilitate peeling.

BOIL: To cook a food in water or other liquid at 212° F. A full rolling boil is essential for cooking some foods (such as pasta) but undesirable for cooking others (such as stocks).

CARAMELIZE: To cook sugar or another food in a sauté pan or saucepan over direct heat long enough to allow the sugar, or the sugar in the food, to begin to brown. Caramelizing imparts a brown color and a nutty flavor to the finished dish.

CLARIFIED BUTTER: The butter fat remaining after whole butter is melted until it separates and the milk solids (a milky liquid) are drained off.

DEBEARD: To remove the fibrous strands extending from the hinged side of a fresh mussel. Mussels use these strands to attach themselves to shoreline rocks.

DEGLAZE: To pour a liquid into a cooking pan from which the fat has been removed, apply heat, and remove particles of food remaining in the pan after sautéing or roasting. The liquid may be wine, brandy, juice, stock, or even water.

DICE: To cut foods into small cubes. Generally, small dice is ⅛ inch square, medium dice is ¼ inch square, and large dice is ⅜ to ½ inch square.

DOCK: To pierce raw pastry with the tines of a fork. Steam is produced inside pastry when the butter melts; docking allows this steam to escape, preventing the dough from rising.

EGG WASH: Beaten whole egg, sometimes with water or milk added, that is brushed onto a pastry exterior. When the pastry is baked, the egg browns slightly, producing a glossy, golden-brown appearance.

FOLD: Generally with the help of a rubber spatula, to combine gently two foods, one being highly whipped. This method of blending allows the whipped product to retain its whipped-in air. It is most often associated with soufflés.

FOOD MILL: With the advent of food processors, this ingeniously simple gadget has fallen on hard times. But it can still be a tremendous aid in pureeing soups and sauces. It consists of a straight-sided container with a perforated bottom. In a small opening in the bottom center rests the shaft, bent out, then up, at 90° angles, with a knob attached to the top end. A curved flange attached to the shaft presses against the perforated bottom. To operate the mill, you pour a soup or sauce into the container and turn the crank. The flange presses the soup or sauce through the perforated bottom as a puree.

JULIENNE: To cut into strips ranging from ⅛ by ⅛ by 1 inch to ¼ by ¼ by 2 or 3 inches. Or any food cut into such strips.

MINCE: To chop a spice, herb, or vegetable very fine.

MONTÉ: From the French verb *monter*, "to lift," this term refers to the technique of incorporating butter into a sauce or soup just before it is served. Stirring in butter in small pieces creates an emulsion that slightly thickens the liquid and improves or "lifts" the flavor of the final product.

PARISIENNE SCOOP: Commonly known as a melon baller, this tool creates spherical garnishes from fruits and vegetables.

POACH: To cook gently in simmering liquid, at 190° to 200° F.

REDUCE: To decrease the volume of a sauce or stock by simmering or boiling, thus increasing its flavor and thickness.

RENDER: To melt bacon, fatback, chicken fat, or other fat by cooking it in a heavy-gauge pan over medium heat.

SAUCEPAN: A heavy-gauge round cooking vessel with vertical sides and a single handle.

SAUTÉ: From the French verb *sauter,* "to jump." To cook food in a small amount of fat or oil.

SAUTÉ PAN: A round cooking vessel with sloping sides and a single handle.

SCALLOP: Though this term is used most commonly to name the connector muscle of one variety of bivalve mollusk, it is also the English counterpart of the French *escalope* and the Italian *scallopine*—all translations of the Latin word for a slice of meat, game, poultry, or fish, pounded very thin, then cooked.

SIEVE: A fine-screened strainer through which sauces and other foods are pressed, usually with the help of a rubber spatula. Pushing mousses, pâtés, and other finely pureed preparations through a sieve eliminates any remnants of sinew or elements not fully pureed.

SKILLET: A heavy-gauge cast-iron pan with a single handle. Sometimes called a Griswold pan, it can be placed in the oven, thus doubling as a roasting pan.

STEEL: A long, thin, abrasive tool used to maintain a sharp cutting edge on knives—not to be confused with a sharpening stone, which is used to grind a sharp edge. The end of a steel is magnetized to hold any metal burrs removed from a knife's cutting edge.

WHITE PEPPER: Black pepper that has been soaked in water, then rubbed to remove the skin and thin outer pulp. White pepper is preferred over black pepper in some dishes because of its lighter color. Dedicated cooks often keep two pepper mills, one filled with black pepper, the other with white, and each labeled accordingly.

ZEST: The outer, pigmented skin of lemons, limes, oranges, and grapefruits. The oils in the zest give a dish a pungent aroma of citrus. Zest is best removed using a zester, a small, five-holed skinning tool. You can also use a sharp paring knife or a vegetable peeler to shave off strips and then cut these into very fine julienne. If you use this method, however, take care to remove only the outermost skin of the citrus fruit, without any of the underlying white pith.

A NOTE ON THE WINE RECOMMENDATIONS

The wine recommendations included in this book reflect some of our preferences and should be used as basic guidelines only. When it comes to the ideal match, various elements such as the age of the wine, the intensity of flavors and the personal style of the chef, the sommelier, or the winemaker come into play to create a (subjectively) perfect meal.

Just as the dishes in *A Taste for All Seasons* can be interpreted in many ways, wines, too, differ according to many variables—among them, where the grapes are grown (the type of climate, the composition of the soil, etc.) and the kind of care exercised throughout a wine's production. To remain faithful to the regional nature of the dishes, readers should focus on wines from growing areas or varietals native to their own locations. For this reason, the wine recommendations are generic.

We have not made any recommendations for wines to accompany the dessert items. A fine dessert wine, whether it be muscat, sauternes, or port, should be able to stand alone, although late harvest Rieslings and gewürztraminers do harmonize well with fruit desserts.

Classic combinations are a great starting point, but experimentation is the real key to success. Never be afraid to challenge your palate or your guests with a new flavor sensation. You may be responsible for the food and wine trend of the nineties.

RANDALL GOODMAN
Sommelier
Carnelian Room, San Francisco

A TASTE
FOR ALL SEASONS

Stocks

The French term for stock is *fond,* literally, "bottom," referring to the fact that good *fonds* are indispensable to cooking.
For that reason, *fonds* are called the foundation of good
cooking.

Many of the dishes in this collection of recipes call for
stock, so a guide to preparing rich, clear, flavorful stocks is
an appropriate preliminary. Remember, however, that this is
an individual interpretation. Every cook, chef, or cuisinier
has his or her own unique style, which extends to the preparation of stocks. We urge you to explore variations and
develop your own style with stocks, as with all cooking.

Stocks are divided into two primary categories: *brown stock
(fond brun)* and *white stock (fond blanc).* In a brown stock,
some of the ingredients are browned by roasting before they
are added to the stock pot. This imparts a brown hue and
rich flavor to the stock. In a white stock, the ingredients are
assembled without browning.

The ingredients of a stock are divided into three elements:
nutritional, aromatic, and liquid. The nutritional element
consists of meat and bones. The aromatics are divided into
two further categories: *mirepoix*—onions, celery, and
carrots—and *bouquet garni*—a congregation of herbs and
spices, most commonly bay leaf, peppercorns, thyme sprigs,
and parsley stems. The liquid element is water, sometimes
augmented with wine, pan drippings, and/or lemon juice.

Stocks, either white or brown, can be created from any of
the following types of bones: beef, veal, chicken, turkey, duck,
lamb, or game. Fish bones also can be used, but for white
stock only, since they require only one-and-a-half hours simmering time to yield their flavors fully. On occasion, one may
have odds and ends of several varieties of bones. With the
exception of fish bones, these may be combined to create one

all-purpose stock possessing some of the flavor of each of the ingredients.

Regardless of the types of bones used, they should always be washed well with cold water before they are subjected to heat. After washing, the bones will be placed in a stock pot, in the case of white stock, or roasted and then placed in the pot, in the case of brown stock. A thin coating of tomato paste is often spread over bones before roasting to add character and color and aid in the clarification process.

For both white and brown stock, always begin with cold water, which allows the maximum extraction of flavor. Beginning with hot water prematurely seals the pores in the nutritional elements, hindering the full extraction of flavor and nutrients. As a rule, one should add enough cold water to rise above the highest bone by four inches. The stock is then brought just to a boil.

Simmering is vital to stock preparation: the vigorous activity of a boiling liquid prohibits the slow, careful collection of impurities, resulting in a cloudy stock, while slow, gentle simmering promotes clarification, producing a rich, clear liquid. Albumin, a water-soluble simple protein found in animal bones and tissue, as well as in vegetables and egg whites, is an essential part of the natural clarifying process. As the stock simmers, heat convection causes the liquid to move rhythmically around in the pot, while the heat causes the naturally occurring albumin to coagulate, collecting microscopic impurities as the stock moves through it. As the albumin rises to the top of the stock, it should be carefully ladled off and discarded periodically during the cooking process.

Once the first skimming is completed, the aromatic elements are added. In white stock, mirepoix and bouquet garni are added raw; in brown stock, they are roasted, often in the same pan in which the bones were roasted. The mirepoix is also sometimes augmented with the dark green tops of leeks, and some professionals may add a garlic clove as well. Additional herbs may also be included, perhaps a small piece of mace. But there isn't much room for too many other aromatics. A stock pot is not a receptacle for last night's leftover green beans or for odds and ends of vegetable trimmings. The final stock will only be as good as the ingredients from which it is created.

Four hours is the minimum simmering time, though more is recommended—six to eight hours on a small scale. In large commercial kitchens, a stock begun in a sixty-gallon stationary steam kettle may continue uninterrupted for two to three days. Stock is drawn as needed from a built-in spigot near the bottom of the kettle, and water is added at the top to replace what has been taken. When all the flavor of the stock elements has been extracted, the stock is drained, the elements removed and discarded, and the process begins all over again.

At the end of the cooking period, the stock is strained—carefully, since the liquid is still very hot. The straining utensil should be at least as fine as a screen strainer.

The stock must then be cooled to room temperature before refrigerating. Without proper cooling, a stock may sour, its warm, dark, moist environment being a potential breeding ground for bacteria. For this reason, it is a good idea to expedite the cooling step. Place the container of strained stock in a sink full of cold water and ice cubes, and stir the stock periodically. When the stock is cooled, cover the container, and store it in the refrigerator.

Once it has fully chilled in the refrigerator, the stock may have a gelatinous consistency (this gelatin comes from the bones). Any fat still present in the stock will rise to the top and congeal under refrigeration. This can easily be lifted from the top and discarded.

White Stock (Chicken)

6 pounds chicken bones, necks, and backs
1 whole chicken (optional)
1 large Spanish onion, peeled and cut into eighths
1 large carrot, top removed, scrubbed, and roughly chopped
2 stalks celery, rinsed and roughly chopped
1 leek, green top only, well rinsed, and roughly chopped
2 bay leaves
3 sprigs fresh thyme
1 bunch parsley stems
1 teaspoon white peppercorns, cracked

- Thoroughly rinse the bones (and chicken, if used) in cold water.
- Place the bones (and chicken) in a stock pot, and cover them with cold water, 3 to 4 inches above the highest bone. Bring just to a boil, then turn down to a simmer.
- Skim the top, removing fat and impurities.
- Add the vegetables, herbs, and spices.
- Simmer 1 hour. If used, lift out the whole chicken, and set

The optional chicken is included for additional flavor. If you have no particular need for extra chicken meat, simply use some additional bones instead.

Have you ever noticed the rich, clear, savory broth in the soups in many Oriental restaurants? It may be due to the following technique, learned by the author from a Chinese cook. When the water first comes to a simmer, pour the contents of the pot into a colander, discarding the liquid. Rinse the bones in cold water, then begin all over again. A stock made from bones rinsed in this manner will be clear and savory if it is carefully simmered throughout the remaining cooking time.

Any caramelized bits of meat or vegetables stuck to the roasting pan can be removed by "deglazing," a technique by which a liquid is poured into the pan and heated, loosening the caramelized bits, which can then be removed. We often use an all purpose dry red wine, which imparts a rich color and flavor and, because of its acidity, aids in the clarifying process.

it aside to cool. Remove all the meat and skin, reserving the meat for another dish, and return the skin and bones to the simmering stock. Continue simmering, skimming off and discarding impurities periodically.

- Strain, cool, cover, and refrigerate the stock.

Brown Stock (Veal or Beef)

6 to 8 pounds veal and/or beef marrow bones
1 small can tomato paste
2 medium Spanish onions, peeled and cut into eighths
2 medium carrots, tops removed, scrubbed, and roughly chopped
2 stalks celery, rinsed and roughly chopped
1 leek, green top only, well rinsed, and roughly chopped

1 garlic clove, crushed
2 well-ripened tomatoes, rinsed, cored, and roughly chopped
2 bay leaves
3 sprigs fresh thyme
1 bunch parsley stems
2 teaspoons black peppercorns, crushed

- Preheat an oven to 400° F.
- Rinse the bones in cold water. Roast for 30 minutes.
- Spread a light coating of tomato paste over the bones, and roast another 10 minutes.
- Place the bones in a stock pot, and add enough cold water to rise approximately 4 inches above the highest bone. Bring to a boil, turn down to a simmer, and skim.
- Place the vegetables and tomatoes in the roasting pan, and roast 30 minutes, stirring frequently. Add them to the stock, along with the herbs and spices. Simmer 4 to 8 hours, skimming periodically.
- Strain, cool, cover, and refrigerate.

Fish Stock

5 pounds fresh white fish
  bones
1 medium Spanish onion,
  peeled and cut into
  eighths
1 stalk celery, rinsed and
  roughly chopped
1 leek, green top only, well
  rinsed, and roughly
  chopped
3 or 4 mushrooms, rinsed
  and roughly chopped

4 tablespoons (½ stick)
  butter
1 cup dry white wine
juice of 1 lemon
1 bay leaf
1 sprig fresh thyme
1 sprig fresh dill
1 bunch parsley stems
½ teaspoon white
  peppercorns, crushed

- Soak the bones in cold water for 1 hour. Drain, and rinse them.
- Place the onions, celery, leeks, and mushrooms in a stock pot with the butter. Cover, and sauté for 10 minutes over a medium flame. Add the bones, and sauté another 5 minutes.
- Add the wine, lemon juice, and enough cold water to rise 4 inches above the highest bone. Bring to a boil, and turn down to a simmer. Skim, discarding the impurities from the top of the stock.
- Add the herbs and spices, and continue simmering for 1½ hours.
- Strain, cool, cover, and refrigerate.

Sauces

Sauces have changed drastically in recent years, veering far from the traditional approaches to sauce making. The *mother sauces,* five elementary sauces that originated in seventeenth-century France, have served as the foundation for generations of chefs and sauciers all over the world. They still play a role in the basic structure of sauce making, but the whole process of sauce making has advanced and matured.

Other sauces under the French banner also retain their importance yet have undergone transformation: cold sauces, commonly known as salad dressings, based on mayonnaise and vinaigrette; dessert sauces, some thickened with cornstarch or arrowroot, others made *à la carte* (to order) with a base of egg yolks (see the note to Fruit Sabayon, Summer, Final Courses, page 89); and butter sauces (*beurres blancs*). And, beyond the traditional French contributions, there are other sauces from other cultures, different not only in their actual makeup but in their application to the foods they accompany. These, too, have been considered, experimented with, and ultimately incorporated into the scheme of things.

One of the primary elements of recent changes in sauce making relates to thickening agents. Some sauces traditionally are thickened with some form of starch. In three of the five mother sauces, a *roux,* a combination of flour and clarified butter, is employed; in *sauce espagnole,* or brown sauce, for example, the thickening agent is a brown roux, darkened through cooking, when the naturally occurring sugar in the flour caramelizes. This browning fortifies the color of the final sauce and adds a nutty flavor. The espagnole is then combined with an equal volume of brown stock and reduced by half, producing the next refinement, *demi-glace*—*demi* in reference to the reduction by half, and *glace,* French for "mirror," in reference to the sheen produced by the reduction.

Thickening a sauce with starch is not the only option, however, and other alternatives have gained favor in recent years. Often, the flour is omitted, and thickening is achieved instead through *natural reduction*—a process whereby a stock is simmered until it has reduced by as much as 75 percent. The resultant liquid is slightly thick and rich in flavor and sheen, simply by virtue of its concentration. Herbs, aromatic vegetables, wines, brandies, and pan juices released during roasting are then added to this stock, further fortifying its character and flavor. Many of the dishes in this book call for sauces achieved by natural reduction. For dishes requiring a demiglace, a recipe can be found at the end of this chapter.

The next two mother sauces, *velouté*—literally, "velvet" —and *béchamel*—white, or cream, sauce—are also traditionally thickened with a roux, this time, unbrowned. In their place, too, have come natural reductions. A white stock simmered with various aromatics produces a facsimile of velouté. Heavy cream, reduced with aromatics, produces a cream sauce. In the case of heavy cream, recent public health awareness, especially with regard to dietary fats, dictates that we consider fat content. Still, a small portion of a rich sauce as an accompaniment to an occasional entrée seems acceptable if the product represents integrity from a culinary point of view.

Another type of sauce is *beurre blanc* or *beurre rouge,* commonly referred to as butter sauce. These sauces consist of a liquid element—wine, stock, fruit juices, pan drippings —substantially reduced with the addition of various aromatics, then enriched with whole butter, which creates a thickened sauce. In a *beurre blanc,* the liquid may be white wine, lemon juice, white stock, or a combination thereof; in *beurre rouge,* red wine, brown stock, dark fruit juice, and the like are used. Many of the sauces in this book employ this method.

The culinary professionals who shared their recipes for this project have demonstrated their ingenuity in their innovative sauces: a crab wonton is embellished with plum chutney; a special locally fermented vinegar accompanies smoked baby chicken; homemade blackberry ketchup is served with lamb loin; a cranberry relish enhances a dish of cured salmon; rhubarb compote highlights wild duck; an avocado salsa accents a salmon steak; a sweet and pungent shallot compote complements a veal loin. All of these accompaniments are in lieu of traditional sauces.

The subject of sauces is considerable, rich in culture and history—some sauces are named after personalities or designate historic events—and impossible to condense into a brief discourse. We suggest working with the dishes in this book, seeking to understand each dish and its accompanying sauce, one by one, until you have developed your own unique repertoire.

Demi-glace

1 carrot, top removed, scrubbed, and roughly chopped
1 medium Spanish onion, peeled and roughly chopped
1 stalk celery, rinsed and roughly chopped
1 small leek, well rinsed and roughly chopped
1 garlic clove, crushed

¼ cup vegetable oil
1 gallon brown veal or beef stock, hot
1 cup tomato puree, or ½ cup tomato paste
1 bunch parsley stems, tied together with string
2 sprigs fresh thyme
2 bay leaves
1 teaspoon black peppercorns, crushed

- Sauté the vegetables in the oil in a 2-gallon stock pot until they are well caramelized. Add the stock and remaining ingredients. Simmer until reduced by half (1 to 2 hours).
- Strain the stock into a small saucepan, discarding the aromatics. Simmer, and reduce once again by half.
- Strain again into a smaller pan. Continue reducing until the demi-glace is thick and rich. Strain, cool, cover, and refrigerate until ready to use.

SPRING

First Courses

COLD APPETIZERS

Columbia River Caviar Mousse, Lime Sauce

Twelve to Sixteen Servings

FOR THE MOUSSE

vegetable oil as needed

2 packages (2 tablespoons) unflavored powdered gelatin

½ cup cold water

1½ pounds cream cheese, room temperature

2 cups heavy cream, whipped to stiff peaks

3 ounces black sturgeon caviar

1 small Bermuda onion, minced

2 hard-boiled eggs, minced

2 bunches fresh chives, minced

1 loaf white bread, sliced very thin, crust removed

FOR THE LIME SAUCE

1½ cups mayonnaise

5 tablespoons lime juice

¾ cup light cream or half-and-half

salt and pepper as needed

FOR SERVING

4 tablespoons each sturgeon and salmon caviar

4 wedges lime, skinned and seeded

8 sprigs fresh chives

TO PREPARE THE MOUSSE

- Lightly coat the inside of a 9- or 10-inch springform pan with vegetable oil.
- Place the cold water in a small saucepan, and, while slowly stirring, sprinkle in the gelatin. Do not allow lumps to form.

Mousse is a somewhat broadly interpreted member of the French family of farces (a term derived from the verb farcir, *meaning "to stuff"). Unlike pâtés and terrines, mousses are almost exclusively prepared cold or frozen; they are also, more often than not, sweet. Uncooked, whipped egg yolks and whites constitute the binding agent, augmented with unflavored gelatin.*

Technically speaking, this dish is more of a cake than a mousse, since it contains bread, which acts as a stabilizer, absorbing liquid within the dish and giving it body.

- Place the pan over a low flame, and continue stirring until the gelatin is completely dissolved. Pour the mixture into a small bowl, and allow it to cool to room temperature.
- Beat the cream cheese with a whip or with a small hand electric mixer until it is soft and smooth.
- Strain the dissolved gelatin into the cheese, and stir until well blended.
- Fold the whipped cream into the cheese-gelatin mixture until it is completely blended. This is the mousse base.
- Divide the mousse base roughly equally into five bowls. Leave the mousse in one bowl plain. To each of the remaining four bowls, add one of the garnishing elements: caviar, onion, egg, and chives. Gently stir each mixture until blended.
- Cover the inside bottom surface of the springform pan with bread slices, trimming as needed to piece together a solid layer of bread.
- Top the bread with the caviar mousse, using a flexible rubber spatula to spread the mousse evenly. Top this with a layer of bread, then *gently* press down to compact. Top with the onion mousse, followed by another layer of bread, once again pressing down to compact. Top with the egg mousse, then a layer of bread, press down to compact, then with the chive mousse and a layer of bread. Press down one last time to create compact layers.
- Finally, top with a layer of plain mousse. Refrigerate overnight.
- When ready to serve, dip a clean kitchen towel into very hot water, wring it out, then wrap it around the outside of the springform pan for 15 seconds. Run a paring knife around the inside of the pan, then release the outside rim. Return the mousse to the refrigerator to rechill, then prepare the sauce.

TO PREPARE THE LIME SAUCE
- In a small bowl, blend the mayonnaise, lime juice, and cream until smooth. Season to taste with salt and pepper.

TO SERVE
- For each serving, gently place a wedge of mousse on a serving plate, and surround it with about ¼ cup of the sauce. Garnish with the caviars, a lime wedge, and chive sprigs.

Wine recommendation: chilled vodka

A blood orange is a small, sweet variety of orange with a slightly rough-textured skin and ruby-red flesh and juice.

Coriander is one of the oldest cultivated spices, dating back to 5000 B.C. Its seeds have been found in ruins on the Aegean islands and in the tombs of the Pharaohs, and it is known to have been grown by the Assyrians and Babylonians. Used by ancient and modern cultures throughout Europe and the British Isles, it became a mainstay in Latin American cooking after the Spaniards introduced it to the New World.

An anomalous member of the carrot family, coriander differs from its brethren in that its seed is not perishable and that both seed and leaf are used as spices. The upper part of the plant, often referred to by its Spanish name, cilantro, *bears two opposed kinds of leaves and two opposed types of flowers. Completely different from its seed, the flavor and aroma of the leaves are unique among herbs, variously likened to those of rubber, citrus peel, a mixture of cumin and caraway, and honey.*

Whichever is correct, the flavor of cilantro is lively and spirited. The leaves are best used fresh—when dried, they lose virtually all of their punch. Used abundantly in Chinese and Italian cuisines, as well as Spanish and South American, cilantro is also referred to as Chinese or Italian parsley. It should, however, never be confused with flat leaf parsley.

Seviche, Barbary Coast Style

Four Servings

¾ pound sea scallops, each sliced into three rounds
4 tablespoons lemon juice
2 tablespoons lime juice
4 blood oranges
¼ cup medium-diced red bell pepper
¼ cup medium-diced green bell pepper
⅓ cup paper-thin-sliced Bermuda onion
1½ teaspoons minced jalapeño pepper
2 tablespoons minced fresh cilantro
4 large lettuce leaves (Boston or green leaf)

- Combine the scallops with the lemon and lime juice. Marinate them overnight in the refrigerator.
- With a sharp knife, score around the center of 2 of the oranges. Slip the end of the handle of an ordinary spoon into the incision, separating the skin from the orange. Set the four resulting orange cups aside, and squeeze the juice from the leftover pulp. Set this aside.

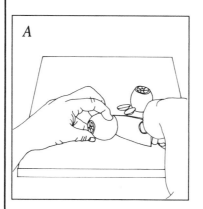

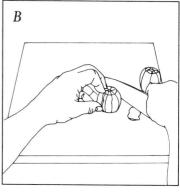

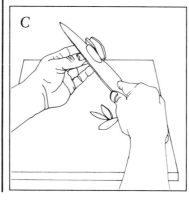

Slice both ends from an orange (A). Slice the peel away from the flesh, removing all the pith (B). Remove the segments by slicing on both sides of the skin that separates them (C).

- Using a sharp knife, completely remove the peel and pith from the remaining two oranges, then extract the segments by cutting on either side of the skin that separates them. Set the segments aside.
- When ready to serve, drain the scallops, and add to them the reserved orange and the bell pepper, onion, jalapeño pepper, and cilantro.
- Fill the orange cups with the scallop mixture, then place each filled cup on a lettuce leaf on an appropriate serving plate.

Wine recommendation: dry gewürztraminer or dry Riesling

Great Lakes Caviar with Potato Pancakes

Four Servings

FOR THE PANCAKES

1 pound new or red
   potatoes, peeled
4 large eggs
¾ cup light cream or half-
   and-half

¼ teaspoon salt
¼ teaspoon pepper
⅓ cup clarified unsalted
   butter

FOR SERVING

4 small new or red
   potatoes, skins on,
   cooked in boiling salted
   water until tender
3 ounces salmon caviar
3 ounces sturgeon caviar

3 ounces whitefish Peppar
   caviar
¼ cup sour cream
1 tablespoon minced fresh
   chives

TO PREPARE THE PANCAKES

- Cook the potatoes in a pot of boiling salted water until tender. Drain.
- Place the potatoes in a bowl, and mash with a masher tool, or whip with a hand electric mixer. Add the eggs, cream, salt, and pepper, and blend thoroughly.
- Cooking 3 or 4 at a time and using about 2 tablespoons of batter for each one, lightly brown the pancakes on both sides in the clarified butter. Repeat until all the batter is used (it should yield 12 or more 2-inch pancakes.)

TO SERVE

- Slice the potatoes into thirds. For each serving, place 3 slices on an individual serving plate. Top each slice with a different variety of caviar. Garnish with 3 potato pancakes, a dollop of sour cream, and a sprinkling of chopped chives.

Wine recommendation: champagne or sparkling chardonnay

Great Lakes Caviar with Buckwheat Mini-crêpes

Four Servings

FOR THE CRÊPES

1 large egg	pinch pepper
1 large egg yolk	2 cups milk
¼ cup buckwheat flour	1 tablespoon melted butter
pinch salt	

FOR SERVING

¼ cup sour cream	3 ounces whitefish Peppar
1 tablespoon grated Spanish	caviar
onion	1 tablespoon minced fresh
3 ounces salmon caviar	chives
3 ounces sturgeon caviar	

TO PREPARE THE CRÊPES

- Whip together the egg, egg yolk, flour, salt, and pepper until smooth. Blend in the milk and melted butter. Cover, and allow to rest in the refrigerator for 1 hour.
- Heat a small nonstick pan over a low flame. Pour in 1 tablespoon of the batter (it should form a circle 4 inches in diameter). Cook until small holes appear on the top surface. Flip, and cook another 30 seconds. Remove to a plate, and repeat until all the batter has been used.

TO SERVE

- Combine the sour cream with the onion. Place a small dollop in the center of each crêpe. Add a small portion of caviar. Roll the crêpe into a cone, pressing it together so that it keeps its shape. Sprinkle with chopped chives, and serve.

Wine recommendation: champagne or sparkling chardonnay

Roast Potatoes and Bell Peppers with Herb Cream

Four Servings

FOR THE POTATOES AND PEPPERS
4 medium potatoes, well scrubbed
1 green bell pepper
1 red bell pepper
1 yellow bell pepper
salt, pepper, and olive oil as needed

FOR THE HERB CREAM
½ cup mayonnaise
2 tablespoons white wine vinegar
1 teaspoon chopped fresh basil
1 teaspoon chopped fresh parsley
1 teaspoon chopped fresh tarragon
salt and pepper as needed
¼ cup light cream or half-and-half

FOR SERVING
4 sprigs fresh chervil or chive

TO ROAST POTATOES AND PEPPERS
- Preheat an oven to 400° F.
- Rub the potatoes and peppers with olive oil. Sprinkle with salt and pepper. Place them on a roasting pan, and roast the peppers for about 30 minutes, or until they begin to turn black. Remove them from the oven, place them in a bowl, and cover it tightly with plastic wrap. Continue roasting the potatoes until tender, then remove them from the oven.
- After 10 minutes, remove the peppers from the bowl. Remove the skin, cut the peppers into quarters, and carefully remove the seeds. Refrigerate both potatoes and peppers until ready to serve.

TO PREPARE THE HERB CREAM
- Thoroughly blend all but the final ingredient. Then, while beating, slowly add the cream. Season to taste with salt and pepper.

Among mild peppers are bull's horns, long, narrow, sickle-shaped green peppers with pointed tips; cubanelles, also known as Cuban peppers, roughly 4 inches long, tapered, either yellow or red; lamuyos, sometimes called European peppers or Rouge Royales, thick-fleshed and longer, larger, and more slender than standard bell peppers; pimentos, heart-shaped red peppers, excellent for roasting and peeling; and sweet banana peppers, long, banana-shaped yellow peppers that also come in a hot variety.

Vinegar is such a basic item in everyday life that we tend to overlook its importance. An indispensable ingredient in mayonnaise, relishes, pickles, condiments, and in the production of candy, it is also used widely for household cleaning and in home health remedies.

More than just a naturally soured apple cider or wine, quality vinegar is created by means of a time-consuming fermentation process that involves the introduction of a special bacteria, called a "mother." (See "Grown in the USA" for a discussion of vinegar.)

Pasta nomenclature often describes some aspect of a given noodle's shape. In the case of linguine, the name comes from the Latin lingua, *meaning "tongue"; linguine, the plural of* linguina, *means "small tongues."*

A small pasta roller cannot produce the long oval-shaped strands that are technically linguine. It can, however, roll a thin strip, a variation of fettucine, technically known as tagliatelle.

Preparing homemade pasta can be time-consuming and labor intensive. Fine fresh pasta is often available in local markets, and there are many good varieties of dried as well. If you do substitute a dried variety, extend the cooking time to roughly 8 minutes (until it is al dente— tender but still firm).

Always make sure that the water in which pasta is to be cooked is boiling vigorously before the pasta is added. If it is not, the pasta will have a mealy consistency.

Similar to sour cream, crème fraîche is a cultured dairy product with a very high fat content. Other recipes for making it call for yogurt and/ or sour cream, as well as buttermilk. We suggest experimenting with several alternatives, using heavy cream as the base, until you arrive at a tartness that suits your palate.

TO SERVE
- For each serving, take a quarter of each kind of pepper and arrange the 3 pieces radially, equally spaced, around a plate. Cut a potato into ¼-inch slices, fan the slices out slightly, and place them in the center of the plate. Drizzle the pepper quarters and potato slices with the herb cream, and garnish with a sprig of chervil or chive.

Wine recommendation: sauvignon blanc

HOT APPETIZERS

Spinach Linguine with Shrimp and Peas

Four Servings

FOR THE PASTA
3 cups semolina flour
2 large eggs
1 tablespoon olive oil
pinch salt

¾ cup fresh spinach, blanched, drained, and pureed

FOR THE CRÈME FRAÎCHE
2 cups heavy cream

¼ cup buttermilk

FOR THE SHRIMP
1 shallot, minced
2 tablespoons olive oil

12 16/20-count shrimp, peeled and deveined

FOR SERVING
1 teaspoon salt
1 tablespoon olive oil

1 cup fresh green peas

TO PREPARE THE PASTA
- Mound the flour on a wooden board. Make a small well in the center, and add the eggs, olive oil, salt, and spinach. Carefully blend together, and knead vigorously, until the dough is smooth and elastic. (If necessary, use additional flour during kneading to prevent the dough from sticking to the board.) Wrap the dough in plastic, and allow to rest in the refrigerator for 1 hour.

- Roll out the pasta dough very thin, using a manually operated pasta roller, then cut the dough into strips, using the fine-strip attachment. Dust strips with flour to prevent them from sticking, and place them on a baking sheet lightly dusted with flour.

TO PREPARE THE CRÈME FRAÎCHE
- Combine the cream and buttermilk in a small saucepan. Heat to 100° F (for best results, use a pastry thermometer to verify that the mixture reaches the requisite temperature), then pour into a bowl. Cover the bowl, and leave in an oven overnight (in a gas oven, the pilot light will generate enough heat to allow the buttermilk culture to grow; in an electric oven, set the thermostat on the lowest possible setting for 2 hours, then turn off).
- Refrigerate the mixture. As it sets, the crème fraîche will rise to the top and grow firm, leaving a bottom layer of whey.

TO PREPARE THE SHRIMP
- Over a medium flame, sauté the shallot in the olive oil for 3 or 4 minutes. Add the shrimp, and sauté another 2 minutes. Blend the crème fraîche into the shrimp. Remove the pan from the fire, and set aside.

TO SERVE
- Bring a gallon of water, the salt, and the olive oil to a rapid boil. Add the pasta, bring back to a rolling boil, and cook for 1 minute. Drain.
- Cook the peas separately in lightly salted boiling water for approximately 2 minutes. Drain and set aside.
- Bring the shrimp mixture to a simmer. Add it to the pasta and peas, toss, and serve.

Dungeness Crabmeat in Phyllo

Four Servings

FOR THE SAUCE

⅓ cup mayonnaise	pinch cayenne pepper
2 tablespoons caper juice	juice of ½ lemon
1 tablespoon minced capers	

Dungeness crab, found in Pacific waters from Alaska to southern California, is unique to the West Coast of the United States. Named after a small town on Washington's Olympic Peninsula, these crabs can measure 10 inches across the body and weigh as much as 3½ pounds.

FOR THE FILLING

2 tablespoons olive oil

2 tablespoons ⅛-inch-diced onion

2 tablespoons ⅛-inch-diced celery

2 tablespoons ⅛-inch-diced carrot

¼ cup heavy cream

½ pound shelled Dungeness crabmeat

juice of 1 lemon

¼ teaspoon cayenne pepper

FOR THE PHYLLO

6 sheets phyllo dough, thawed

¼ cup melted butter

TO PREPARE THE SAUCE

- Combine all the ingredients and blend them together well. Refrigerate until ready to serve.

TO PREPARE THE FILLING

- Sauté the vegetables in the olive oil for 4 or 5 minutes. Add the heavy cream, and reduce by one-third. Place this mixture in a bowl with the crabmeat, lemon, and cayenne, and mix well.

TO PREPARE THE PHYLLO

- Preheat an oven to 350° F.
- Brush 1 sheet of phyllo dough lightly with some of the melted butter. Top this with another sheet of dough. Butter this sheet lightly, and top it with a third sheet and another coating of butter. Cut the layered sheets into 4 strips lengthwise. Repeat with the remaining 3 sheets of phyllo.
- Place a tablespoon of the filling approximately one inch from one end of a strip of dough. Fold one corner of the dough triangularly over the filling. Continue folding this triangle all the way to the end of the strip (see diagram). Repeat this process with remaining strips. Brush with melted butter.
- Place the triangles on a lightly buttered baking sheet, and bake for 4 to 6 minutes, or until golden brown. Serve hot on individual plates accompanied by the sauce.

Wine recommendation: rich chardonnay

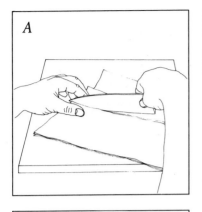

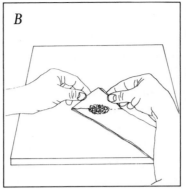

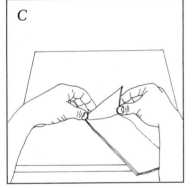

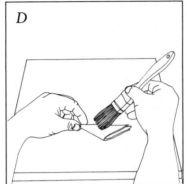

Cut the phyllo dough sheets lengthwise into 4 strips (*A*). Fold a corner of each strip over the crab filling (*B*). Fold the first triangle up along the strip (*C*). Brush the triangle with melted butter (*D*).

Dungeness Crab Wontons, Plum and Ginger Chutney

Eight Servings

FOR THE CHUTNEY

1½ oranges, peeled, segments removed from membrane, and chopped

½ cup fresh-squeezed orange juice

¼ cup granulated sugar

1 heaping tablespoon peeled and minced fresh ginger root

2 tablespoons dried currants

1 teaspoon ground cloves

2 tablespoons water

1 teaspoon curry powder

½ cup apricot preserves

2½ pounds Santa Rosa (or other variety) freestone plums, pitted and cut into ½-inch cubes

Chutney is a corruption of the Sanskrit word chatni, meaning "to lick." These relishes traditionally have been served as accompaniments to other primary courses. Cooked chutneys consist of underripe fruits simmered with sugar, vinegar, and aromatics such as chili peppers, ginger, and garlic. One of the most popular of these is Major Grey's Chutney—an indispensable accompaniment to curry—made of chunks of crunchy mango. Fresh chutneys may use a base of yogurt, flavored with herbs such as mint or cilantro. Recently, chutneys have enjoyed a considerable revival in restaurants, where they are found in an infinite variety— from pineapple to sun-dried tomato, from pear and raisin to tomatillo and jalapeño.

FOR THE WONTONS

1 cup heavy cream
1 tablespoon butter
2 tablespoons minced onion
½ stalk celery, minced
1 pound Dungeness
   crabmeat, roughly
   chopped

1 tablespoon chopped fresh
   cilantro
¼ teaspoon soy sauce
pinch freshly ground pepper
40 4-by-4-inch egg-roll
   skins
vegetable oil for deep frying

FOR SERVING

4 large sprigs flat leaf
   parsley

TO PREPARE THE CHUTNEY

- Place all of the ingredients except the plums into a small saucepan. Bring to a boil, and simmer for 30 minutes.
- Add the plums, and simmer for another 15 to 30 minutes, or until the plums are soft. Cool, cover, and refrigerate.

TO PREPARE THE WONTONS

- Simmer the cream in a small saucepan until it is reduced by half.
- Sauté the onion and celery in the butter for 3 or 4 minutes. Place in a mixing bowl, and toss with the cream, crabmeat, cilantro, soy sauce, and pepper.
- Draw an imaginary line from corner to corner across a wonton skin. Place a level teaspoon of the filling in the center of the skin, to one side of the imaginary line. Dip a finger in water, and moisten the edges of the skin. Fold the skin on the imaginary line, pressing the edges together.
- Grasp the two corners on either side of the fold with the forefinger and thumb of each hand. The fold should be up. Moisten the back of one of the corners being held, turn the two corners up, and press them tightly together (see diagram). Repeat this procedure with the remaining skins.
- Pour two inches of vegetable oil into a heavy-gauge pot. Heat to 360° F. Deep-fry the wontons until they are golden and crispy. Drain on absorbent paper.

TO SERVE

- If served as an appetizer course, place 5 wontons on a plate, accompanied by the chutney, and garnish with a sprig of flat leaf parsley.

Wine recommendation: dry Riesling or dry gewürztraminer

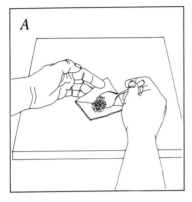

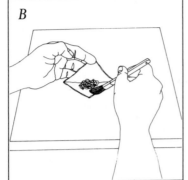

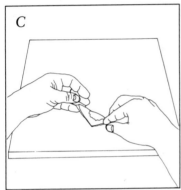

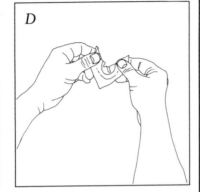

Place a small amount of filling onto each wonton skin (*A*). Moisten the edges of the wonton skin with water (*B*). Fold the wonton over, pressing the edges together (*C*). Fold the corners up (*D*), and press them together (*E*).

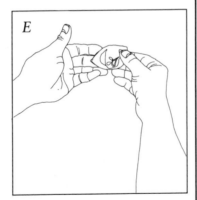

Corn Crêpes
with Asparagus and Smoked Salmon

Four Servings

FOR THE CRÊPES

4 large eggs
¾ cup flour
¾ cup cornmeal

pinch salt
pinch pepper
2 cups milk

Asparagus reportedly was called "sparrow grass" in England up until the eighteenth century. A member of the lily family (along with leeks and onions) and related to grasses, asparagus is believed to be native to Eurasia. Its structure is unique among vegetables in that it does not possess leaves in the ordinary sense; instead, it has phylloclades, photosynthetic branches that develop in clusters near the tip of the stalk.

Asparagus is difficult to cultivate, taking up to three years to yield a crop. The stalks also grow at different rates, requiring even more careful cultivation. This investment of time and labor may explain their high retail cost.

FOR THE GLAZE
1½ cups heavy cream

4 ounces Tillamook cheddar cheese, grated

1 large egg yolk

dash Tabasco sauce

FOR ASSEMBLY
12 asparagus spears, cut into 6-inch lengths, peeled, and blanched in slightly salted water

½ pound smoked salmon, sliced paper-thin

TO PREPARE THE CRÊPES
- In a small bowl, beat the eggs, flour, cornmeal, salt, and pepper until smooth.
- Blend the milk thoroughly into the mixture. Allow to rest 1 hour.
- Heat a 6-inch nonstick pan over a low flame. Pour in enough batter to coat the bottom of the pan thinly. When the top surface is nearly dry, flip the crêpe, and cook it another 30 seconds. Remove the finished crêpe, and set aside on a plate. Repeat until all the batter has been used, stacking crêpes on the plate as they are cooked. The batter should yield 12 crêpes.

TO PREPARE THE GLAZE
- Bring the cream to a simmer. Transfer to a food processor or blender. Add the cheese, egg yolk, and Tabasco, and puree.

TO ASSEMBLE
- Preheat an oven to 375° F.
- Place 1 asparagus spear and a slice or two of smoked salmon on a crêpe. Roll up, and place in a lightly buttered oven-proof casserole dish (you may wish to place 3 crêpes in each of four individual casserole dishes). Top with the cheese mixture, and bake uncovered for 8 to 12 minutes, or until golden brown.

Wine recommendation: rich sauvignon blanc or light chardonnay

SOUPS

Back Bay Mussel Chowder

Four Servings

2 pounds mussels, scrubbed
   and debearded
1 cup dry white wine
1 medium Spanish onion,
   cut into ¼-inch dice
2 garlic cloves, minced
2 pinches saffron
1½ pounds tomatoes,
   peeled, cored, seeded, and
   cut into ¼-inch dice

1 cup bottled clam juice
2 pounds potatoes, peeled
   and cut into ¼-inch dice
salt and pepper as needed
4 sprigs fresh dill

- Place the mussels and wine in a pot, cover, and simmer for about 5 minutes, or until all the shells open. Remove the mussels, separate the meat from the shells, discard the shells, and set the meat aside.
- Add the onion, garlic, saffron, tomatoes, and clam juice to the wine. Simmer, uncovered, for 5 minutes. Add the potatoes, and continue simmering for 8 to 10 minutes, or until the potatoes are tender.
- Add the mussel meat to the simmering broth. Season the soup to taste with salt and pepper. Serve, garnished with dill.

Wine recommendation: sauvignon blanc

Puree of Split Pea with Dungeness Crab

Four to Six Servings

½ cup ¼-inch-diced slab
  bacon
1 stalk celery, roughly
  chopped
1 medium Spanish onion,
  roughly chopped
¼ carrot, peeled and
  roughly chopped
2 cups green split peas,
  rinsed

1 bay leaf
1 small smoked ham hock,
  cut into thirds
1½ quarts chicken stock
½ cup heavy cream
1 cup Dungeness crabmeat
salt and pepper as needed
1 cup toasted croutons

- Place the diced bacon in a heavy-gauge soup pot, and render over a medium flame until brown and crispy.
- Add the celery, onion, and carrot. Cover, and sauté for 8 to 10 minutes. Add the peas, bay leaf, ham hock, and chicken stock. Simmer gently, stirring frequently, for 1 hour.
- Remove the ham hocks. Separate the meat from the bone, and cut it into ¼-inch pieces. Set it aside.
- Puree the soup in a food processor (this may need to be done in small batches). Then return the soup to the pot, and add the cream, ham hock meat, and crab. Bring to a simmer, and season to taste with salt and pepper. Serve garnished with the croutons.

Wine recommendation: dry Riesling

SALADS

Warm Leek Salad

Leeks often carry sand or soil in between their leaves. Be sure to wash them thoroughly, two or three times.

Four Servings

8 medium leeks, white part
  only (about 4 inches long)
water as needed

1 garlic clove, sliced
1 teaspoon salt
¾ cup olive oil

FOR SERVING

salt and freshly ground
  black pepper as needed

a fresh baguette or loaf of
  French bread

- Carefully cut the root from the end of each leek; the leaves should remained joined. Split each leek in half, and gently rinse several times in cold water, making sure that the leeks do not come apart.
- Place the leeks and water to cover in a saucepan, along with the garlic, salt, and about half of the olive oil. Cover, and simmer for about 12 minutes. Remove from the fire, allow to sit for 10 minutes, then drain the leeks thoroughly.

TO SERVE

- For each serving, place 4 leek halves on a plate, cut side down. Drizzle some of the remaining olive oil over them, sprinkle lightly with salt and pepper, and serve with a piece of warmed French bread.

Wine recommendation: dry Riesling

Steamed Asparagus, with Chive Sauce and Red Pepper Puree

Four Servings

FOR THE PUREE

2 red bell peppers
olive oil as needed

3 tablespoons chicken stock
  (or water)

FOR THE SAUCE

1 small shallot, minced
1 bay leaf
1 small garlic clove, minced
1 tablespoon olive oil
½ cup dry white wine

2 tablespoons heavy cream
16 tablespoons (2 sticks)
  unsalted butter, at room
  temperature
salt and pepper as needed

FOR ASSEMBLY

24 thin asparagus spears,
  cut evenly into 4-inch
  lengths

1 tablespoon minced fresh
  chives

Nomenclature for peppers can be confusing, since there are numerous varieties, and some are called by different names in different regions. In the United States, mild peppers are known as sweet, or bell, peppers; hot peppers are called just that, or chilies. In England, all peppers are called chillies, the hotter varieties being termed hot chillies. In Latin America, mild peppers are called pimentos, and hot ones are chilies.

Peppers are a rich source of Vitamin C, containing more than is found in citrus fruit and six to nine times that found in equivalent amounts of tomatoes. They also contain as much Vitamin A as carrots.

The heat in hot peppers/ chilies depends on how much capsaicin is present. This alkaloid accumulates in the fruit as the pigment develops during ripening. It is concentrated mostly in the internal connective tissue and the placental tissue; there is considerably less in the flesh and seeds. Thus, by removing the connective tissue, one can regulate a pepper's heat. Because of capsaicin's pungent properties, it has many other uses. For example, it is an important ingredient in some external muscle liniments, in homemade insecticides, and in antidog and antimugger sprays.

TO PREPARE THE PUREE
- Preheat an oven to 400° F.
- Rub the peppers lightly with olive oil. Place on a baking sheet, and roast until they begin to turn black. Remove from the oven, place in a bowl, and cover tightly with plastic wrap. Allow to sit 10 to 15 minutes.
- Cut open the peppers, and separate the skin and seeds from the flesh. Discard the seeds and skin.
- Puree the peppers and the chicken stock in a blender or food processor. Set the puree aside, keeping it warm.

TO PREPARE THE SAUCE
- Sauté the shallot, bay leaf, and garlic in the olive oil for 3 or 4 minutes. Add the wine, and simmer until almost dry. Add the cream, and bring the sauce back to a simmer.
- Add the butter, roughly 2 tablespoons at a time, stirring continuously until all the butter is incorporated. Strain, season to taste with salt and pepper, and set aside in a warm place.

TO ASSEMBLE
- Place the asparagus in lightly salted boiling water, and simmer 3 or 4 minutes, or until tender but still firm. *Be careful not to overcook.* Drain.
- Add the chopped chives to the sauce, then ladle it onto 4 warm serving plates. Lay 6 asparagus spears on the sauce on each plate, then place 3 tablespoonfuls of the pepper puree around the asparagus.

Spring Greens, Illinois Brie, and New York State Foie Gras

Four Servings

FOR THE VINAIGRETTE
2 tablespoons olive oil
6 tablespoons vegetable oil
¼ cup raspberry vinegar
⅛ teaspoon salt
⅛ teaspoon freshly ground black pepper

FOR THE SALAD

a variety of fresh seasonal
    greens sufficient for 4
    salads (arugula, Boston
    lettuce, red leaf lettuce,
    radicchio, mache, endive,
    spinach, chicory, etc.)

4 1-ounce slices New York
    State Foie Gras
3 tablespoons vegetable oil
4 ½-inch-thick wedges
    Illinois Brie cheese

FOR SERVING

12 ¼-inch-thick slices
    French bread, toasted

TO PREPARE THE VINAIGRETTE

• Combine all the ingredients in a small bowl, and whip them
  together vigorously. Set aside.

TO PREPARE THE SALAD

• Preheat an oven to 350° F.
• Tear all of the salad greens into bite-size pieces. Rinse well
  in cold water, and drain. Wrap in absorbent paper, or dry
  in a salad spinner, then place in the refrigerator.
• Heat the vegetable oil to the smoking point in a small sauté
  pan. Sauté the foie gras slices about 10 seconds on each
  side, until slightly browned.
• Place the brie wedges on a small baking dish, and warm
  them in the oven for 2 minutes.
• Place the salad greens in a mixing bowl, add the vinaigrette,
  and toss.

TO SERVE

• Arrange the greens on 4 individual chilled salad plates. Place
  a slice of warm foie gras and a wedge of warm brie on top
  of each salad. Set 3 slices of toasted French bread on the
  side of each plate.

Wine recommendation: Pinot Noir

Frederick Kolb, a German immigrant, founded the Kolb Cheese Company in Muscatine, Iowa, in 1898. After being forced to relocate five times because of insufficient milk supplies, Mr. Kolb finally settled in Lena, Illinois, in 1925, remaining president of the firm (renamed the Kolb-Lena Cheese Company) until his death in 1942. Karl Renter, Kolb's son-in-law, took over operation of the company, and, in 1951, he introduced a new type of Swiss cheese, which had been developed at Iowa State University. To this day, Delico Baby Swiss remains one of the company's most popular items.

Karl Renter passed away in 1962, and his wife, Frieda, took over as new president. Between 1969 and 1987, the company changed ownership three times. It is currently owned by the European based group, Bongrain.

Essentially to suit American palates, the Illinois Brie produced by Kolb-Lena is considerably milder than similar European cheeses. However, it will take on a stronger character if it is left out to ripen for several days.

Main Courses

FISH

Striped Bass, California Style

Four to Six Servings

1 5-pound striped bass, gutted and scaled, with head and tail intact
3 stalks fresh fennel, roughly chopped
1 small carrot, peeled and roughly chopped
1 leek, green part only, roughly chopped
1 small Spanish onion, peeled and roughly chopped
1 stalk celery, roughly chopped
6 ripe medium tomatoes, roughly chopped
4 garlic cloves, minced
2 teaspoons crushed black pepper

1 pinch saffron
½ cup Ricard (a bottled aperitif)
6 parsley stems
2 cups dry white wine
2 cups fish stock
4 ounces tomato puree
1 sprig fresh thyme
1 sprig fresh marjoram
1 sprig fresh rosemary
1 bay leaf
3 leeks, white part only, cut into julienne
3 stalks celery, cut into julienne
1 small fennel bulb, cut into julienne

- Preheat an oven to 400° F.
- Butter an ovenproof dish. Place the fish in this dish, along with all of the ingredients except the julienned vegetables. Cover with a sheet of parchment paper cut to the size of the dish, and bake for 30 minutes.

- Carefully pour the juices from the dish into a saucepan. Simmer until reduced by half.
- Add the julienned vegetables to the reduced liquid, and simmer 5 minutes.
- Place the fish on a large serving platter. Top it with the julienned vegetables and some of the reduced liquid. Serve with the remaining liquid on the side.

Wine recommendation: dry chardonnay or Chablis

Steamed Flounder, Saffron and Green Peppercorn Sauce

Four Servings

FOR THE SAUCE
1 large shallot, minced
3 tablespoons olive oil
1 teaspoon mashed green peppercorns

½ teaspoon saffron
½ cup dry white wine
1½ cups heavy cream
salt and pepper as needed

FOR THE FISH
4 7- or 8-ounce flounder fillets
salt and pepper as needed
24 very thin asparagus spears, cut into 5-inch lengths

¾ cup shelled fresh green peas
½ cup dry white wine
½ cup water

TO PREPARE THE SAUCE
- Sauté the shallot in the olive oil for 3 or 4 minutes. Add the peppercorns, saffron, and white wine. Simmer until reduced by half. Add the cream, and continue simmering until again reduced by half. Season to taste with salt and pepper. Set aside, keeping warm.

TO PREPARE THE FISH
- Split each fillet in half lengthwise, and sprinkle lightly with salt and pepper. Roll up each fillet, skin side in, and secure with a toothpick. Place the fillets in a vegetable steaming basket, along with the asparagus and the peas. Set the basket in a saucepan just large enough to hold it, and pour in the white wine and water. Cover the pan, and simmer for 8 minutes, or until the fish is fully cooked.

Saffron, the world's most expensive spice, is the dried stigmas of a variety of crocus. Its high cost is due not only to the painstaking labor required to remove the stigmas, flower by flower, but also to the number of stigmas it takes to yield one pound of saffron: as many as 300,000.

Saffron probably originated in Asia Minor, Italy, and Greece, and was cultivated as early as 2000 B.C. Its color, an intense orange yellow, has long been considered a symbol of royalty. It was cultivated in the fifteenth and sixteenth centuries for use in dyes, but that practice waned because of saffron's expense. In modern India, however, it is still used to color ceremonial garments and bridal veils.

In spite of its high cost, saffron plays an important role in the cuisine of the American Pennsylvania Dutch. In indulging this extravagant appetite, however, they are merely enjoying the rewards of their own industry, for they raise all of the saffron they consume. Their preference for manual toil and tendency to raise large families furnish the abundant supply of labor necessary to harvest the spice.

The Schwenkfelder family is credited with introducing saffron to Eastern Pennsylvania in the eighteenth century, when they emigrated from Germany, transplanting to American soil the business they had been pursuing in their homeland. A recipe for Schwenkfelder Kuchen, a saffron-flavored cake, can be found in many a Pennsylvania Dutch recipe collection.

- Remove the toothpicks from the rolled fillets. For each serving, place two flounder rolls on a serving plate. Ladle some sauce over the fish, and arrange some asparagus and green peas on the sauce around the fish.

Wine recommendation: buttery chardonnay

Poached Sea Trout, Purple Basil Cream Sauce

Four Servings

4 6-ounce sea trout fillets	1 cup dry white wine
salt and pepper as needed	1½ cups heavy cream
¼ cup melted butter	2 tablespoons unsalted
2 large shallots, minced	butter
4 ripe medium tomatoes,	10 leaves purple basil, cut
peeled, seeded, and diced	into fine julienne
6 large mushrooms, sliced	
1 tablespoon chopped fresh	
parsley	

- Preheat an oven to 350° F.
- Butter an ovenproof baking dish.
- Season the fish lightly with salt and pepper, and place it in the dish.
- Sprinkle the shallots, tomatoes, mushrooms, and parsley over the fish. Drizzle the melted butter over this, and pour in the white wine. Cover the dish, and place it in the preheated oven. Cook for 12 minutes, or until the fish is tender.
- Pour the liquid from the fish into a small saucepan. Simmer until reduced by half. Add the heavy cream, and again simmer until reduced by half.
- For each serving, place a fillet on a warmed plate, top with some sauce, and sprinkle with julienned basil leaves.

Wine recommendation: dry sauvignon blanc

Purple basil is one of possibly a dozen or more different varieties of this member of the mint family. It is preferred here for its color, but its flavor is nearly the same as that of the standard green variety, if you need to make a substitution.

True sea trout is more precisely a fish found in European waters. It is similar to our salmon, in that it returns to spawn in the fresh waters from which it came, often traveling considerable distances to do so. The record for the longest homing run—more than 600 miles—is reportedly held by a Polish sea trout.

Sea trout in the United States is more than likely weakfish, a member of the drum family, so named for the drumming sound they make. The weakfish's name derives from its weak mouth tissues, easily torn by fish hooks. They are found in the Atlantic, from Massachusetts to Florida, close to shore in the summer months and migrating offshore during the winter.

Pan-fried Rainbow Trout

Four Servings

4 rainbow trout, boned
salt, pepper, and flour as
  needed
¼ cup vegetable oil
juice of 1 lemon
4 tablespoons (½ stick)
  butter, cut into ½-inch
  cubes

¼ cup chopped fresh
  parsley
8 slices or 4 wedges of
  lemon
4 large sprigs parsley

- Preheat an oven to the lowest possible setting.
- Remove the head, tail, and dorsal fins from each trout. Open the fish, season on both sides with salt and pepper, then dredge in flour, shaking off the excess.
- Heat the oil in a cast-iron skillet or a nonstick pan over a medium flame. When the oil is hot, place the fish in the pan, skin side up. Sauté until golden brown, turn over, and repeat on the other side. Remove to a baking pan, and place in the oven to keep warm.
- Pour the excess oil from the pan, and discard it. Deglaze the pan with the lemon juice. Stir in the butter until it is fully emulsified. Blend in the parsley, then remove the sauce from the fire.
- Place each trout on a serving plate. Top with sauce, and garnish with lemon and parsley.

Wine recommendation: dry Riesling

SHELLFISH

Sea Scallops, Soy-Ginger Butter

Four Servings

FOR THE BUTTER
¼ cup dry white wine
3 tablespoons grated fresh
  ginger root
1 shallot, minced

2 tablespoons soy sauce
16 tablespoons (2 sticks)
  unsalted butter
salt and pepper as needed

Rainbow trout is one of the most popular of all trout species. But, with the exception of sea-run, or steelhead, rainbow trout, the sale of wild trout is prohibited in the United States. Consequently, domestic production consists of farm-raised fish. These are olive green, speckled with black spots, with silver bellies. Rainbow trout are distinguishable from other varieties by the broad red band running down their sides, though this may not be as evident on the cultivated variety. The fish, generally harvested under one pound, have white or light pink flesh and a slightly nutty flavor.

FOR THE SCALLOPS

1 pound sea scallops
salt, pepper, and flour as
   needed
3 tablespoons clarified
   butter
2 cups stemmed and
   roughly chopped fresh
   spinach leaves

1 ripe tomato, peeled,
   cored, seeded, and cut
   into ¼-inch dice
salt and pepper as needed

TO PREPARE THE SAUCE

- Combine the white wine, ginger, and shallot in a small saucepan. Simmer until almost dry. Add the soy sauce.
- Add the butter, stirring continuously until it is fully incorporated. Strain, and set aside.

TO PREPARE THE SCALLOPS

- Pat the scallops dry with a clean towel. Sprinkle with salt and pepper, and dust them lightly with flour.
- Heat a sauté pan over high heat. Pour in the clarified butter. Sauté the scallops in the butter for 30 seconds on each side. Remove from the pan with a slotted spoon, and set aside.
- Sauté the spinach in the same pan until it is wilted. Season to taste with salt and pepper. Remove from the pan, and set aside.
- Add the tomatoes to the pan, and sauté until nearly dry.
- For each serving, place a small mound of spinach in the center of a serving plate, and ladle about ¼ cup of the sauce around it. Arrange scallops around the spinach, then sprinkle them with diced tomato.

Wine recommendation: dry Riesling

Scallops and Spring Vegetables in Puff Pastry

Four Servings

FOR THE SAUCE

2 large shallots, minced
¼ cup sliced mushrooms
2 tablespoons butter
½ cup dry white wine

¼ cup chicken stock
2½ cups heavy cream
salt and pepper as needed

FOR THE PASTRY

1 package frozen puff
    pastry dough

1 egg, beaten

FOR THE FILLING

1 pound bay or sea scallops
2 tablespoons olive oil
½ cup julienned carrots

½ cup julienned celery
½ cup julienned zucchini
½ cup julienned snow peas

TO PREPARE THE SAUCE

- Sauté the shallots and mushrooms in the butter for about 5 minutes. Add the white wine and stock, bring to a simmer, and reduce until roughly 1 tablespoon of liquid remains. Add the cream, and simmer until reduced by half. Season to taste with salt and pepper. Set aside.

TO PREPARE THE PASTRY

- Preheat an oven to 350° F.
- Cut out 8 2½-inch-wide circles of pastry. Cut out a 2-inch circle from the center of 4 of the 2½-inch circles. (Wrap the 4 2-inch circles, refrigerate them, and save for another use.)
- Brush the surface of each of the 4 uncut circles with beaten egg. Place the rings on top of the circles, and brush them with egg. Place the pastry on a baking sheet, and bake for 20 minutes, or until golden brown. It will have risen an inch or more. Remove from the oven, and set aside.

TO PREPARE THE SCALLOPS

- Sauté the scallops in the olive oil over high heat for 30 seconds on each side. Remove them from the pan with a slotted or perforated spoon, and set them aside. Sauté the julienned vegetables over high heat in the same pan for 2 or 3 minutes. Remove about a quarter of the vegetables,

A scallop is a bivalve mollusk found in North America on the Atlantic and Gulf coasts. The edible part is the white abductor muscle that holds together the fan-shaped, fluted shells. Sea scallops are roughly five inches across, with an edible muscle about one inch wide and a half-inch thick; bay scallops—which are not baby sea scallops but a distinct variety of shellfish— are about two inches across, with a half-inch muscle.

The scallops found in the bay waters around Nantucket Island, located off the southern coast of Cape Cod, are particularly prized for their sweetness and tenderness. The commercial season for Nantucket Bay scallops runs from November through April, though in some years the growth cycle dwindles, shortening the season to as few as two months (November and December). The daily limit per harvester is ten bushels, yielding approximately seventy pounds of edible scallops. An experienced shucker can shuck one and a half to two bushels of scallops an hour.

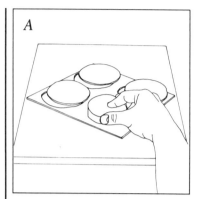

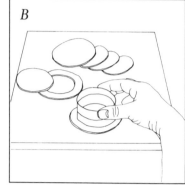

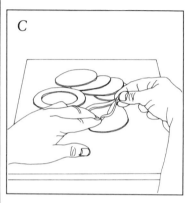

Cut out 8 2½-inch-wide circles of puff pastry (A). Cut out a 2-inch circle from the center of each of 4 of the 2½-inch circles (B). Brush the surface of each of the 4 uncut circles with beaten egg, place a pastry ring on top of the circle, then brush again with beaten egg (C).

and set them aside. Add the sauce to the vegetables remaining in the pan, and bring it to a simmer. Add the scallops, simmer them for a minute, and season to taste with salt and pepper.

• Place the pastry shells on serving plates, and fill them with the scallop and vegetable mixture. Sprinkle each one with some of the reserved vegetables.

Wine recommendation: chardonnay

POULTRY

Smoked Roasted Baby Chickens, Red Wine Vinegar Sauce

Four Servings

FOR THE CHICKEN

½ cup salt

⅓ cup granulated sugar

2 quarts cold water

5 whole cloves

2 teaspoons juniper berries, crushed

3 tablespoons black peppercorns, crushed

4 tablespoons honey

4 bay leaves

½ orange, roughly chopped

½ lemon, roughly chopped

4 boneless baby chickens (*poussins*), trimmed of excess fat and wings

2 tablespoons olive oil

FOR THE SAUCE

1 shallot, minced

1 garlic clove, minced

1 bay leaf

¼ cup dry red wine

¼ cup red wine vinegar

16 tablespoons (2 sticks) unsalted butter

salt and pepper as needed

TO PREPARE THE CHICKEN

- Combine all the ingredients except the chicken and the olive oil, and stir until the salt, sugar, and honey are dissolved.
- Immerse the chickens in this brine, and allow them to marinate for 3 hours.
- Remove the chickens, and pat them dry. Place them on a rack set in a pan, and refrigerate overnight.
- Place the chickens in a small smoker, and follow the manufacturer's directions for use. The chickens should be lightly smoked, about 30 minutes.
- Preheat an oven to 350° F.
- Sauté the chicken in the olive oil, skin side down, until lightly browned. Then place it skin side up in a roasting pan, and roast for 10 minutes.

TO PREPARE THE SAUCE

- Combine the shallot, garlic, bay leaf, red wine, and vinegar in a small saucepan. Simmer until reduced by half.
- Add the butter about 2 tablespoons at a time, stirring continuously after each addition to incorporate it fully into the sauce. Strain, and season to taste with salt and pepper.

Smoking is a centuries-old technique used to preserve meat, fish, poultry, and game. Items to be smoked are generally soaked for one to two days in a liquid brine consisting of water, salt, sugar, and various aromatic vegetables, herbs, and spices. For the smoking, hardwoods such as oak, hickory, and alderwood are preferred over more resinous woods and may be augmented with herbs or spices such as rosemary, laurel, thyme, juniper, cinnamon, liquorice, cloves, and so on.

Smoking is not the same as cooking; temperatures must be low enough to allow the smoke to permeate the items being smoked without cooking them. In a "cold-smoke," the temperature generally does not exceed 80° F, allowing for a longer smoking period, while, in a "hot-smoke," temperatures may run as high as 150° F.

The cook who does not have access to a smoking device may skip the smoking step, which will make the brining process unnecessary as well. If you choose this option, simply follow the method of preparation for the chicken, but allow 30 minutes or more for roasting.

If baby chickens are unavailable, you may wish to substitute fresh chicken breasts or Cornish game hens, available in the freezer section of most supermarkets.

- Ladle the sauce onto 4 serving plates, then place a smoked chicken on top of each. Serve with one or two seasonal vegetables, such as steamed broccoli flowerettes and thinly sliced carrots sautéed in butter.

Wine recommendation: light Pinot Noir or Beaujolais

Breast of Chicken with Pesto Mousse

Four Servings

Pesto is a Genovese concoction of basil, olive oil, garlic, and grated Parmesan, Romano, and/or Pecorino cheese. Its name derives from pestle, *the wooden or stone instrument traditionally used to pound the mixture to a paste in a wooden or stone mortar.*

2 fresh 2½- to 3-pound chickens, split in half, with wings removed	¼ teaspoon pepper
	1 cup heavy cream
	8 large or 16 medium spinach leaves, well rinsed
3 tablespoons pesto	
¼ teaspoon salt	

- Using a sharp boning knife, cut away and remove the bones from each breast. Then, for each chicken half, grasp the breast with one hand, and carefully work the other hand between the skin and the meat of the thigh. Peel the skin from the entire leg by gently pulling on the breast while slipping the other hand farther down the leg. At the end of the drumstick, the skin should slip smoothly off the leg. It should remain intact and attached to the body. Cut the skinned leg from the body at the thigh joint, then cut the meat from each leg, discarding the bones (or saving them for a stock).
- Cut the chicken leg meat into ½-inch cubes, place in a bowl, and freeze for about an hour, or until half frozen. Chop into very small pieces in a food processor. Return to the bowl, and freeze for another hour.
- Return the chopped chicken to the food processor. Add the pesto, salt, and pepper, and puree until a smooth mass forms. While adding the cream slowly, continue pureeing until the mixture is smooth and well blended.
- Preheat an oven to 375° F.
- Lay the chicken breasts skin side down on a counter. Pound them gently, then place a quarter of the spinach leaves and a quarter of the mousse on each one. Fold the breast meat over the spinach leaves and mousse.
- Enclose each breast half in its attached leg skin by carefully turning the skin inside out over it. (If you were thorough about folding the meat over the mousse and spinach, the

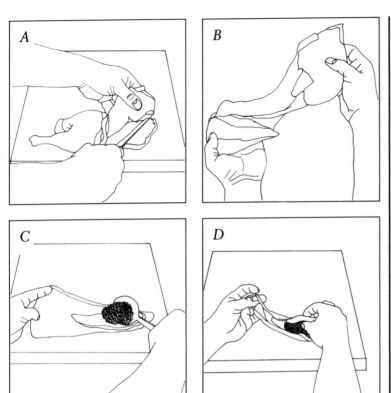

Remove the bones from the inside of the breast (*A*). Grasp the breast, with the skin attached, and pull it back, peeling the skin from the leg (*B*). Place the spinach, then the mousse, onto the pounded breast (*C*). Turn the leg skin inside out to enclose the breast (*D*).

job should not be messy.) Tuck the skin neatly around the breast to make a nicely rounded form. Place the breasts in a lightly buttered baking pan, with the gathered edges of skin facing down. Roast 25 minutes, or until golden brown.

Wine recommendation: Pinot Noir or soft merlot

One of the hundreds of varieties of cheese made in Switzerland, Gruyère is named after the valley in which it is manufactured, located in the canton (province) of Fribourg. In the United States, "Swiss" is a generic term, referring to any cheese with characteristic holes that is about 30 to 40 percent water, 30 percent fat, and 25 percent protein. The holes are created by the release of carbon dioxide gas by one of the starter bacteria early in the formation of the cheese.

Breast of Chicken with Gruyère

Four Servings

4 6- to 8-ounce chicken breasts, boned and lightly pounded
salt, pepper, and flour as needed
2 large eggs
¼ cup milk
2 cups plain bread crumbs
½ cup vegetable oil
2 ripe tomatoes, peeled, and cut into 6 slices each

8 ½-ounce slices Gruyère cheese
4 tablespoons (½ stick) butter
1 cup sliced mushrooms
½ teaspoon flour
1 cup dry white wine
¼ cup chopped fresh parsley

- Preheat an oven to 350° F.
- Season the chicken breasts lightly with salt and pepper, and dust lightly with flour. Beat the eggs and milk together. Dip the breasts into this mixture, then coat them with the bread crumbs.
- Heat the oil in a skillet or sauté pan, and sauté the breaded chicken until golden brown on both sides. Top each breast with 3 slices of tomato, then with 2 slices of Gruyère. Put the chicken in a baking pan, and place it in the oven until the cheese is melted.
- In the meantime, pour off the excess oil from the pan, and discard it. Heat the butter until melted, then sauté the mushrooms. Sprinkle in the flour, and blend it in well. Stir in the white wine, and simmer until the sauce is smooth and thickened.
- When the cheese has completely melted, place each chicken breast onto a serving plate, and top with the sauce. Sprinkle each serving with chopped parsley.

Wine recommendation: merlot or light zinfandel

LAMB

Stir-Fried Lamb with Chicago Noodles

Four Servings

1 pound lamb loin, trimmed of fat and sinew and cut into ¼-inch julienne	⅓ cup vegetable oil
	1 stalk bok choy, cut on the bias into ⅛-inch slices
1 tablespoon very finely julienned fresh ginger root	12 shiitake mushrooms, stemmed and cut into ¼-inch julienne
1 tablespoon minced jalapeño pepper	3 tablespoons minced flat leaf parsley
2 tablespoons soy sauce	¾ cup chicken stock
3 tablespoons sesame oil	1 teaspoon arrowroot (or cornstarch)
½ pound rice noodles or vermicelli	4 sprigs flat leaf parsley

- Combine the lamb, ginger, pepper, soy sauce, and 1 tablespoon of the sesame oil in a bowl, and allow to marinate for 1 hour.
- Drop the rice noodles into 1 gallon of boiling salted water. Bring the water back to a boil, and cook the noodles for 3 minutes. Drain them very well, separate into 4 equal portions, and set aside.
- Heat the vegetable oil in a cast-iron skillet over a medium flame. Place one portion of the rice noodles in the pan. Form into a rough cake, and fry on both sides until golden brown. Drain on absorbent paper, and set aside, keeping warm. Repeat with the remaining portions of noodles.
- Heat a wok over a high flame. Add 1 tablespoon of sesame oil. Add the bok choy, shiitakes, and minced parsley, and stir-fry for 1 minute. Remove, and set aside.
- Drain the lamb, reserving the marinade. Add the last tablespoon of sesame oil to the wok, then stir-fry the lamb for 2 minutes. Return the vegetables to the wok, and add the chicken stock.
- Dissolve the arrowroot in the reserved marinade. When the stock comes to a boil, stir in the dissolved starch. Bring the mixture back to a boil, then remove from the fire.
- Place each portion of fried noodles on an individual serving

Arrowroot is a highly refined root starch, manufactured from a West Indian plant. Cornstarch, a similar product, also highly refined, is manufactured from corn seed. In cooking, their application is different from that of the traditional roux *(flour plus fat). Both are correctly dissolved in cold liquid, then added to a simmering sauce, stew, or stir-fry. Either one requires only 30 seconds to achieve its maximum thickening effect and adds a welcome sheen to the finished product. Cornstarch is commonly employed in Chinese cooking, but, again, its use is strictly a matter of taste.*

plate. Top with some of the stir-fry and sauce, and garnish with a sprig of flat leaf parsley.

Wine recommendation: spicy zinfandel or soft cabernet sauvignon

Lamb Medallions, Saffron Butter

Four Servings

A compound butter is softened whole butter combined with herbs, spices, and/or liquid flavorings, then shaped and chilled. Slices placed atop grilled meats and fish serve as an alternative to traditional sauces.

The saffron butter can be prepared a day or two before serving. Any remaining saffron butter can be wrapped airtight and stored almost indefinitely in the freezer.

FOR THE BUTTER

1 shallot, minced	1 sprig fresh thyme
1 garlic clove, minced	salt and pepper as needed
1 cup dry white wine	12 tablespoons (1½ sticks)
½ teaspoon saffron	unsalted butter, softened
1 small bay leaf	

FOR THE LAMB

4 4½-ounce lamb loin steaks, pounded to a ½-inch thickness	salt and pepper as needed
	2 tablespoons olive oil
	2 tablespoons vegetable oil

TO PREPARE THE BUTTER

- Place all the ingredients except for the butter in a saucepan. Simmer until reduced to approximately 3 tablespoons. Remove the bay leaf and thyme, and discard them.
- Place the butter in a food processor. Add the reduced liquid, and blend thoroughly.
- Place the butter on a sheet of wax paper, and shape it into a rough cylinder. Wrap the wax paper around the butter, then, with a ruler, press the paper firmly against the butter to create an even and smooth cylinder. Twist the ends of the paper shut, and store in the refrigerator until ready to serve.

TO PREPARE THE LAMB

- Season the lamb medallions with salt and pepper. Sauté in the oil to the desired degree of doneness, browning well on both sides. Remove to appropriate serving plates.
- Cut 4 ¼-inch slices of the butter. Remove the wax paper from the slices, then place one on each of the lamb medallions. Serve with a steamed seasonal vegetable.

Wine recommendation: cabernet sauvignon or heavy red Burgundy

Rack of Lamb, Pinot Noir Sauce

Four Servings

1 rack of lamb, split and frenched, with chine bones removed	2 tablespoons Pernod
	½ cup Pinot Noir
	1 cup beef stock
salt and pepper as needed	1 small bay leaf
1 small shallot, minced	1 teaspoon cornstarch
½ tablespoon butter	2 teaspoons cold water
1 tablespoon chopped fresh tarragon	1 small bunch fresh watercress

- Preheat an oven to 350° F.
- Season the lamb with salt and pepper. Sauté it meat side down over high heat until it is light brown. Place in the oven, and roast for 20 to 25 minutes, turning over once. Remove from the oven, and set aside in a warm place.
- Sauté the shallot in the butter for 4 or 5 minutes. Add the tarragon, Pernod, and wine. Simmer until reduced by one third. Add the stock and bay leaf, and reduce by half.
- Dissolve the cornstarch in the water. Add it to the sauce, and simmer briefly until the sauce has thickened. Strain.
- Cut the 2 half-racks into 4 double chops each. Ladle the sauce onto 4 serving plates, and arrange 2 double chops on each plate. Garnish with watercress.

Wine recommendation: cabernet sauvignon or heavy red Burgundy

"Frenched" refers to a technique by which all connective meat is removed from the rib bones, which are scraped clean with a knife. The chine bone, which is part of the backbone, must be removed so that the racks can be cut into chops. Both of these steps can be performed by your local butcher.

The word ketchup *has its origins in the Chinese word* ketsiap, *a pickled fish sauce of ancient origin. In England in the seventeenth century,* ketchup *referred to a fermented sauce made from mushrooms and walnuts. Tomato ketchup is a pickle of sorts. Since tomato is considered a fruit botanically, it follows that a liquid pickle could be created from any fruit, such as the blackberry ketchup innovated here.*

Steamed Lamb Loin, Blackberry Ketchup

Four Servings

FOR THE KETCHUP

1 12-ounce jar of seedless blackberry jam
½ cup cider vinegar
½ teaspoon ground cinnamon
1 teaspoon grated fresh ginger root

½ teaspoon ground allspice
pinch ground cloves
pinch black pepper
½ teaspoon salt

FOR THE LAMB

2 lamb loins, boned and skinned, with all fat and sinew removed
salt and pepper as needed
12 small new potatoes, scrubbed and cut in half
4 slices fresh ginger root

24 spears thin asparagus, cut into 4- or 5-inch lengths
8 morel or shiitake mushrooms, stems removed

TO PREPARE THE KETCHUP

• Bring all the ingredients to a boil in a small saucepan, and simmer for 20 minutes, stirring frequently. Remove from the fire, and allow to cool.

TO PREPARE THE LAMB

• Season the lamb loins with salt and pepper. Place in a steamer basket along with the potatoes. Pour an inch of water into a pan just large enough to accommodate the steamer, and add the sliced ginger. Set the steamer in the pan, bring the water to a boil, cover the steamer, and simmer for 15 to 20 minutes. Remove the lamb, potatoes, and mushroom caps, and set aside in a warm place.
• Place the asparagus and the mushrooms in the steamer basket. Cover, and steam for 3 to 5 minutes, or until tender. Remove from the fire.
• Slice the lamb loins, and arrange the slices on 4 appropriate serving plates. Arrange the asparagus, potatoes, and mushroom caps next to the sliced lamb. Serve accompanied by the blackberry ketchup.

Wine recommendation: cabernet sauvignon or heavy red Burgundy

Final Courses

COLD DESSERTS

Chocolate Brownie Cheesecake

Sixteen Servings

FOR THE BROWNIES
8 tablespoons (1 stick)   pinch salt
    unsalted butter   1 cup granulated sugar
2 ounces unsweetened   2 large eggs
    chocolate   1¼ cups flour
1 teaspoon granulated   3 tablespoons cocoa
    instant coffee   1 cup chopped walnuts
½ teaspoon vanilla extract   butter and flour as needed
¼ teaspoon almond extract

FOR THE CHEESECAKE
2 pounds cream cheese   4 large eggs
1 teaspoon vanilla extract   graham cracker crumbs as
1⅔ cups granulated sugar   needed (approximately ½
pinch salt   cup)

TO PREPARE THE BROWNIES
- Preheat an oven to 350° F. Lightly butter and flour an 8-inch square baking pan.
- Place the butter and the chocolate in the top half of a double boiler, and melt over barely simmering water, stirring occasionally. Remove from the fire. Add the coffee, extracts, salt, and sugar, and stir until the mixture is smooth and well blended.
- Add the eggs, one at a time, and stir until completely incorporated.

- Sift the flour and cocoa together.
- Blend in the dry ingredients and the nuts.
- Pour the batter into the baking pan, and bake for 25 minutes, or until a toothpick inserted into the center comes out clean.
- Allow to cool in the pan for 10 minutes, then turn out onto a board. Cut into ½-inch cubes, and set aside.

TO PREPARE THE CHEESECAKE
- Using a hand electric mixer, beat the cheese, vanilla, sugar, and salt in a bowl until smooth and creamy. Add the eggs one at a time, incorporating each completely before adding the next.
- Pour half of the batter into a lightly buttered 9- or 10-inch springform pan. Top with the brownie cubes, and pour over the remaining batter. Bake in the 350° F oven for exactly 1¼ hours, or until a toothpick inserted into the middle comes out clean. Cool to room temperature, cover, and refrigerate overnight.
- Unmold the cheesecake. Press cracker crumbs into its sides, and serve.

White Chocolate Mousse Cake, Raspberry Sauce

Sixteen Servings

FOR THE SAUCE
1 pint dry-pack frozen
    raspberries
¼ cup water

¼ cup granulated sugar
3 tablespoons Grand
    Marnier

FOR THE FILLING
12 ounces white chocolate
4 tablespoons (½ stick)
    unsalted butter
1½ tablespoons dark rum
¼ ounce (1 package)
    unflavored granulated
    gelatin

¼ cup cold water
3 cups heavy cream
¼ cup granulated sugar

FOR THE CAKE

½ cup flour
3 tablespoons cocoa powder
4 eggs
½ cup granulated sugar

4 tablespoons (½ stick) unsalted butter, melted and cooled to room temperature

FOR ASSEMBLY

dark chocolate shavings for
 decoration

TO PREPARE THE SAUCE

- Bring the raspberries, water, and sugar to a boil in a small saucepan. Simmer for 15 minutes. Strain the berries through a fine sieve. Blend in the Grand Marnier. Cover, and refrigerate until ready to serve.

TO PREPARE THE FILLING

- Combine the chocolate, butter, and rum in the top half of a double boiler. Heat over barely simmering water, stirring occasionally, until the chocolate is melted and the ingredients are smooth and well blended. Remove from the fire, and allow the mixture to cool.
- Pour the cold water into a small saucepan, and sprinkle in the gelatin. Heat until the gelatin is dissolved. Blend into the chocolate mixture. Set aside.
- Whip the cream with a hand electric mixer, sprinkling in the sugar while beating, until the cream forms stiff peaks.
- Fold half of the whipped cream into the chocolate mixture until it is smooth and well blended. Refrigerate the plain whipped cream.

TO PREPARE THE CAKE

- Preheat an oven to 300° F. Butter and flour a 10-inch cake pan, and set it aside.
- Sift the flour and cocoa together. Set aside.
- Blend the eggs and sugar in a stainless steel mixing bowl. Set this over a simmering water bath, making sure that it does not touch the water. Using a whisk, whip the egg-sugar mixture until it has tripled in volume, approximately 5 minutes. Remove the bowl from the water bath, and beat another 8 to 10 minutes with a hand electric mixer until the mixture is light, fluffy, and cool.
- Slowly mix in the melted butter, then slowly fold in the flour-cocoa mixture, until well blended. Do not overmix.
- Pour the batter into the prepared cake pan. Bake 20 to 25

The tropical cocoa tree, a native of South America, has been cultivated and its fruit enjoyed by many indigenous tribes. Its botanical name is Theobroma cacao—the Greek theobroma meaning "food of the gods" and cacao being a Spanish corruption of the the the Aztec cacahuatl, "cacao beans." The word chocolate, however, derives from the Aztec word for "bitter water." The Aztecs believed that Quetzalcoatl, their god of wisdom and knowledge, bestowed upon them this plant with its bitter-tasting bean. That the cacao bean was used as a form of currency by South American natives is an indication of its cultural importance. Europeans were first introduced to it when Columbus brought some beans back to Spain after his fourth transatlantic voyage in 1502.

Dr. James Baker of Dorchester, Massachusetts, built the first chocolate factory in the United States in 1765. It wasn't until 1893 that Milton Snavely Hershey was inspired to venture into the chocolate manufacturing business by an exhibit at the Chicago Exposition. Today, Hershey, Pennsylvania, is generally considered the chocolate capital of the United States.

minutes, or until a toothpick inserted in the center comes out clean.
- Immediately turn the cake onto a cake rack to cool.
- When the cake is cool, use a serrated-edge knife to slice it horizontally into thirds.

TO ASSEMBLE
- Place one round of sponge cake into a 10-inch springform pan, and spread half of the chocolate mousse on top of it. Place the second round of the cake on top of this, and spread with the remaining half of the mousse. Top with the third round of cake. Cover, and chill at least 1 hour.
- Remove the cake from the pan, and spread the top and sides with the plain whipped cream. Sprinkle the chocolate shavings on top. Chill for another half hour or so. Serve accompanied by the raspberry sauce.

WARM DESSERTS

Doughnut and Raisin Bread Pudding

Four to Six Servings

Bread pudding evolved as a way to use up stale bread (doughnuts, in this case). Properly seasoned, it can be an excellent dish.

If you are concerned about calories or fat content, substitute low-fat milk for the cream and plain vegetable oil, such as safflower, for the butter.

6 day-old plain or sugar-glazed doughnuts	1 cup half-and-half
¼ to ½ cup granulated sugar	4 ounces raisins
	½ teaspoon cinnamon
4 large eggs	pinch freshly grated nutmeg
	butter as needed

- Preheat an oven to 300° F.
- Break the doughnuts into ½-inch pieces, and place these in a bowl. Add the sugar, adjusting the amount according to the sweetness of the doughnuts.
- Beat the eggs to a froth in a separate bowl. Add the half-and-half, raisins, and spices, and beat until blended.
- Pour this mixture into the doughnuts, and stir.
- Pour this mixture into a lightly buttered ovenproof baking dish. Bake for 30 minutes. Serve warm.

Spiced Rice Pudding

This pudding can also be served cold.

Four Servings

1 quart milk
¼ cup raw long-grain white
  rice
½ cup seedless raisins
½ cup granulated sugar
2 tablespoons orange zest
1 tablespoon lemon zest

½ tablespoon grated fresh
  ginger root
⅛ teaspoon freshly grated
  nutmeg
⅛ teaspoon ground cloves
1 teaspoon vanilla extract
½ teaspoon salt

- Preheat an oven to 300° F.
- Blend all the ingredients together in a bowl. Pour into a lightly buttered casserole dish. Bake 2½ hours, uncovered, stirring every half hour. Serve warm.

Warm Strawberry and Apple Compote, Raspberry Sauce

Four Servings

FOR THE SAUCE
1 pint dry-pack frozen
  raspberries
¼ cup granulated sugar

½ cup water
2 tablespoons Chambord

FOR THE COMPOTE
1 tablespoon unsalted butter
2 tablespoons granulated
  sugar
½ cup dry white wine
½ vanilla bean, split
  lengthwise

2 Granny Smith apples,
  peeled, cored, and cut
  into 12 wedges each
1 pint fresh ripe
  strawberries, cleaned,
  hulled, and sliced

FOR SERVING
4 whole strawberries

4 sprigs fresh mint

TO PREPARE THE SAUCE
- Combine the raspberries, sugar, and water in a small saucepan, and simmer for 10 minutes. puree in a blender or food processor, along with the Chambord, then strain through a fine sieve. Set aside.

TO PREPARE THE COMPOTE
- Bring the butter, sugar, wine, and vanilla bean to a boil in a small saucepan. Add the apples, and simmer, covered, for about 5 minutes, until they are tender but still firm.
- Add the sliced strawberries, cover, and simmer for 1 minute.

TO SERVE
- Arrange the apples and strawberries on 4 individual serving plates. Surround each serving with the raspberry sauce, and top with a whole strawberry and a sprig of mint.

CAKES AND BREADS

Banana Nut Bread

Banana is interesting among fruits. Native to India and Malaya, it is a distant relative of ginger. Botanically a berry, in fifteenth- and sixteenth-century Europe, it was known as the "Indian fig."

When picked in an unripe state, the banana is almost entirely starch. But, as it ripens off the vine, this starch turns to sugar, up to 20 percent by weight.

This recipe calls for a very ripe banana. One that has begun to turn brown would be perfectly acceptable; texture is irrelevant since the banana is incorporated into the bread.

1 Loaf

8 tablespoons (1 stick) unsalted butter, softened	1 teaspoon salt
⅔ cup granulated sugar	½ cup chopped pecans and/ or walnuts
2 large eggs	1 cup chopped dates and/or raisins
3 tablespoons milk	1 cup very ripe, mashed banana
2 cups flour	butter and flour as needed
1 teaspoon baking powder	
½ teaspoon baking soda	

- Preheat an oven to 350° F. Lightly butter and flour a 9-by-5-inch loaf pan.
- Beat the butter and sugar together with a hand electric mixer until light and fluffy. Beat in the eggs, one at a time. Blend in the milk.
- Sift the dry ingredients together. Beat them into the creamed mixture until the batter is smooth. Fold in the nuts, dried fruit, and banana.
- Pour the batter into the loaf pan. Bake for 1 hour, or until a toothpick inserted into the center of the loaf comes out clean.

SUMMER

First Courses

COLD APPETIZERS

The cranberry, the largest species of a number of tart red berries native to North America and Europe, is unique to North America. Smaller varieties are called the foxberry in England and, in various parts of the United States, the red whortleberry, partridge berry, whimberry, mountainberry, rockberry, and cowberry (the Latin word for cow being vacca *and the botanical name for the American cranberry,* Vaccinium macrocarpon*).*

Gin-cured Salmon, Horseradish Sauce and Cranberry Relish

Eight to Twelve Servings

FOR THE SALMON
2 cups salt
¾ cup granulated sugar
3 tablespoons crushed black peppercorns
6 tablespoons crushed mustard seeds
1 2- to 3-pound fresh salmon fillet, skin on

1 cup gin
1 cup whole fresh cranberries, crushed
1 orange, unpeeled, sliced very thin

FOR THE RELISH
zest of 1 orange
1 tablespoon unsalted butter
6 tablespoons granulated sugar
1 cup dry sherry

1 cup dry white wine
½ cup fresh-squeezed orange juice
2 cups whole fresh (or fresh-frozen) cranberries

FOR THE SAUCE
¾ cup gin
¼ cup juniper berries
1½ cups mayonnaise
½ cup half-and-half or light cream

2 tablespoons distilled white vinegar
¼ cup prepared horseradish
pinch salt
pinch pepper

FOR SERVING
zest of 1 orange, cut into
   very fine julienne
juice of 1 lemon

1 cup water
12 sprigs flat leaf parsley

TO PREPARE THE SALMON
- Combine the salt, sugar, peppercorns, and mustard seeds in a small bowl.
- Place the salmon fillet in a shallow glass or stainless steel pan, flesh side up. Douse it with ¼ cup of the gin, then sprinkle it with half of the salt-sugar mixture.
- Press the crushed cranberries into the salmon, and cover them with a layer of the thinly sliced orange. Top with the rest of the salt-sugar mixture, and pour on the remaining gin.
- Lay a sheet of plastic wrap over the salmon. Press another, slightly smaller pan down on the fillet. Weigh down this pan with cans or large pebbles. Refrigerate the salmon for 3 days.

TO PREPARE THE RELISH
- Sauté the zest in the butter for 3 minutes. Add the sugar, sherry, wine, and orange juice, and simmer until reduced by half. Add the cranberries, and simmer until the mixture is thick and smooth and the cranberries have all opened. Cover, and refrigerate until ready to serve.

TO PREPARE THE SAUCE
- Bring the gin and juniper berries to a boil, and simmer until reduced by two-thirds. Allow to cool, then strain into a blender or a food processor. Add the mayonnaise, half-and-half, vinegar, horseradish, salt, and pepper, and puree. Refrigerate overnight.

TO SERVE
- Combine the zest, lemon juice, and water in a small pan, and simmer together for 2 minutes. Drain, discarding the liquid, wrap the zest securely, and refrigerate overnight.
- Remove the weighted pan from the salmon, and discard the curing materials.
- Using a long, thin, flexible knife held at a 45° angle in relation to the fish, slice the salmon paper-thin.
- For each serving, cover half of a small serving plate with horseradish sauce. Arrange 4 or 5 slices of cured salmon down the center of the plate, overlapping the sauce. Place

Among the many native dishes to which the Wampanoag Indians introduced the Pilgrims was pemmican, cranberries crushed with dried venison and bear fat, an important food staple for surviving the rugged New England winters. The colonists called the tart red berries "crane berries" because of their delicate pink blossoms, each resembling the head of a crane.

In 1677, when the Massachusetts colonists had the audacity to mint their own coins, they shipped ten crates of cranberries, along with some codfish and Indian corn, to Charles II, then king of England, in an attempt to appease his wrath. In 1787, James Madison wrote to Thomas Jefferson, who was in France at the time, for some background information on constitutional government, for use at the upcoming constitutional convention. Jefferson supplied the requested information in exchange for a shipment of apples, pecans, and cranberries. By this time, cranberries had become so popular in New England that one Cape Cod village levied a fine of one dollar on anyone found picking more than a quart of them before September 20.

a teaspoon of the cranberry relish on the bare side of the plate. Sprinkle orange zest on the salmon. Garnish with flat leaf parsley.

Wine recommendation: dry sauvignon blanc

This is a recent American variation of beefsteak tartare, a dish of minced beef tenderloin, seasoned with salt and pepper, and garnished with raw egg yolk, capers, chopped onion, and parsley. The traditional way to puree the salmon (or the beef) is to mince it with a sharp knife until it is cut very fine. It can also be run through a meat grinder, using first the large-holed plate and then the fine-holed plate. Freezing the grinder attachments before use facilitates the grinding process.

Salmon Tartare Garni

Four Servings

FOR THE SALMON

1 pound salmon fillet, skinned and pin bones removed
¼ cup olive oil
1 anchovy fillet, minced
1 teaspoon capers, minced
1 small shallot, minced

1 teaspoon Dijon mustard
1 garlic clove, minced
juice of ¼ lemon
leaves of 1 sprig thyme, minced
½ teaspoon green peppercorns, mashed

FOR SERVING

12 whole green peppercorns
8 radicchio leaves, cut in half lengthwise
8 sprigs fresh thyme

12 thin slices lemon, seeded
¼ cup salmon caviar
1 small brioche, sliced ¼-inch thick and toasted

- Using a sharp cook's knife, mince the salmon into approximately ⅛-inch pieces. Place it into a mixing bowl.
- Add the remaining tartare ingredients to the salmon, and blend thoroughly. Cover, and refrigerate for 2 to 6 hours.

TO SERVE
- Shape the tartare into 4 oval-shaped patties, and place each one on a chilled serving plate. With a spoon, make a small indentation in the top of each patty, and place in it 3 peppercorns and a tablespoon of salmon caviar. Garnish as desired with radicchio leaves, lemon slices, thyme, and toasted brioche.

Wine recommendation: dry sauvignon blanc

Chilled Barbecued Quail
with Fettucine and Pickled Vegetables

Four Servings

FOR THE PICKLED VEGETABLES

2 cups assorted vegetables (pickling cucumbers, green, red, and/or yellow bell peppers, pearl onions, baby zucchini, yellow, and/or patty pan squash, small whole okra, carrots, cauliflower, Brussels sprouts, etc.), cut into a variety of shapes (julienne, round slices, half slices, slices on the bias, spheres, squares, triangles, flowerettes, etc.)

1 teaspoon salt
1 cup dark brown sugar
½ cup granulated sugar
½ teaspoon turmeric
¼ teaspoon ground cloves
1 teaspoon mustard seeds
1 teaspoon coriander seeds
1 teaspoon black peppercorns
1 bay leaf
1½ cups cider vinegar
½ cup water

FOR THE QUAIL

1 medium Spanish onion, grated
¼ cup vegetable oil
½ cup dry white wine
juice of 1 lemon
½ cup ketchup
2 tablespoons dark brown sugar
2 teaspoons orange marmalade

1 garlic clove, minced
½ teaspoon grated fresh ginger root
1 tablespoon Worcestershire sauce
½ teaspoon dried red pepper flakes
1 teaspoon Tabasco sauce
4 glove-boned quail

FOR SERVING

½ pound dry fettucine
3 tablespoons olive oil
¼ cup chopped fresh parsley

pinch salt
pinch pepper

TO PICKLE THE VEGETABLES
- Place the vegetables in a bowl, sprinkle with the salt, and allow to sit for 3 hours.
- Bring the remaining pickling ingredients to a boil, and simmer for 5 minutes.

Barbecue sauce is a distinctly American innovation, and every region has its own variation. The recipe here is an invention of one of the authors, but he will not be insulted if you prefer to use a sauce of your own creation.

Glove-boning is a process by which a quail's central cavity is cleared of bones, without the bird being cut open. Wing, thigh and leg bones are still intact.

Be sure the water is boiling vigorously before you add the pasta. Otherwise, the pasta will taste mealy.

This dish can also be served warm.

- Rinse the vegetables in cold water. Drain. Place them in the simmering brine, and simmer for 5 minutes. Remove from the fire, allow to cool to room temperature, then refrigerate, covered, for at least 48 hours.

TO PREPARE THE QUAIL
- Preheat an oven to 400° F.
- Sauté the onion in the vegetable oil over a low flame, covered, for 12 minutes. Add the white wine, and simmer, uncovered, until reduced by three-quarters.
- Transfer the pan's contents to a bowl, and blend in the remaining ingredients, stirring until the sugar is dissolved.
- Coat the quail liberally with this barbecue sauce. Place in a roasting pan, and roast 20 minutes, basting frequently with the remaining sauce. Remove from the oven, allow to cool to room temperature, then refrigerate, covered, until chilled.

TO SERVE
- Boil the fettucine in 2 gallons of lightly salted water for 8 to 10 minutes, or until the pasta is al dente (tender but still a bit chewy). Drain, rinse in cold water, and drain again thoroughly.
- Place the fettucine in a bowl. Add the olive oil, parsley, salt, and pepper. Mix well.
- Using a fork, twirl one-quarter of the fettucine into a nest. Place this on an individual serving plate. Repeat with the rest of the noodles.
- Pour a small quantity of barbecue sauce next to each pasta nest. Place a roasted quail on top of the sauce. Garnish with 3 or 4 tablespoons of pickled vegetables.

Wine recommendation: fruity Beaujolais

Goat Cheese Tart
with Leeks and Seasonal Herbs

Four Servings

½ cup finely diced leek, white part only
4 tablespoons (½ stick) butter
1 cup goat cheese
½ cup cream cheese
⅛ teaspoon salt
¼ teaspoon white pepper

1 teaspoon minced fresh chives
½ teaspoon each minced fresh thyme and tarragon
4 large eggs
½ cup sour cream
8 sprigs each chives, thyme, and tarragon

- Preheat an oven to 350° F. Butter an 8-inch tart pan.
- Sauté the leek in 1 tablespoon of the butter for 5 minutes.
- Cream the goat cheese in a small bowl, using a hand electric mixer. Blend in the remaining butter, cream cheese, salt, pepper, and minced herbs until smooth. Add the eggs, one at a time, incorporating each before adding the next. Add the leek and the sour cream.
- Pour the mixture into the prepared pan. Bake 20 to 25 minutes, or until golden brown. Allow to set for roughly 5 minutes before serving.
- Slice the tart into 8 wedges, and serve garnished with the chives, thyme, and tarragon.

Wine recommendation: gewürztraminer

Cheese of all varieties has been an integral part of the human diet for more than five thousand years. Commercially manufactured cow milk cheeses have dominated the U.S. market since the mid-nineteenth century, while goat milk cheese has been limited to small, independent family endeavors.

Making goat cheese is remarkably simple. Unlike most other cheese-making processes, the procedure involves no heating of curds, no pressing of whey from curds, and a modest aging time. The essentials are impeccably clean and fresh milk, attention to detail, and the cheesemaker's skill.

Goat cheese is considerably easier to digest than are other cheeses, and it boasts significant amounts of protein, carbohydrates, vitamins, and minerals—and only 82 calories—per 1-ounce serving.

HOT APPETIZERS

Sea Scallop and Spinach Timbale

Four Servings

1 pound fresh sea scallops
zest of ½ lemon
juice of 1 lemon
juice of 1 lime
1 large garlic clove, mashed

½ jalapeño pepper, minced
1 shallot, minced
1½ pounds fresh spinach, washed and stemmed
butter as needed

Timbale comes from the Arab word thabal, "drum," referring to the small metal receptacle once used to serve guests a welcoming beverage upon their arrival. These timbales were made of silver or gold, plain or ornate, but, over the years, timbale has come to describe all sorts of bowls, made of metal, earthenware, or china.

In a culinary context, a timbale is traditionally any kind of preparation baked and served in a crust or dough, but it has considerably broader applications as well. Cold mousses, vegetable salads, or poached eggs, for instance, encased in aspic—a savory meat-flavored jelly—are also prepared in a timbale mold. Any dish prepared in a small single-serving container, then inverted and served, may be called a timbale.

One of the authors once made a timbale of braised leeks bound with pureed potatoes and encased in leek leaves. The advantage of working with a timbale is that an attractive pattern—of leek leaves, julienned vegetables, or fettucine, for example— can be set into the mold, which is then filled with a compatible filling and, when inverted, reveals the decorative pattern. Layering multicolored ingredients, such as scallops and spinach, as in this dish, shows them off to their best advantage.

- Slice the scallops in half, and combine with the zest, juice, garlic, jalapeño, and shallot. Refrigerate and marinate 24 hours.
- Preheat an oven to 375° F.
- Drop the spinach into boiling salted water. Bring the water back to a boil, and simmer 3 minutes. Drain, and squeeze dry. Butter 4 6-ounce ramekins or soufflé cups.
- Remove the scallops from the marinade, arrange a layer of them in each ramekin, and top with a layer of the spinach. Add another layer of scallops, then another layer of spinach.
- Place the ramekins in a baking pan, and fill it with enough water to reach halfway up their sides. Place in the preheated oven for 8 to 10 minutes.
- Remove the ramekins, dry their outsides, then invert each onto an individual serving plate. Serve accompanied by heated French bread.

Wine recommendation: sauvignon blanc

Beer-battered Shrimp, Apricot-Ginger Coulis

Four Servings

FOR THE COULIS

6 fresh ripe apricots, peeled and pitted	¼ cup fish stock
1 tablespoon grated fresh ginger root	2 dashes Tabasco sauce
	1 dash white Worcestershire sauce

FOR THE SHRIMP

1 quart peanut oil	3 large egg whites
2 12-ounce bottles dark beer	16 U-12 shrimp, peeled and deveined, tails intact
½ teaspoon salt	flour as needed
1 cup flour	4 sprigs flat leaf parsley

TO PREPARE THE COULIS

- Puree all the ingredients in a food processor, then pour into a container, cover, and refrigerate until ready to use.

TO PREPARE THE SHRIMP

- Preheat an oven to 300° F. Heat the peanut oil in a heavy-gauge pan to 360° F.

- Pour the beer into a mixing bowl, and sprinkle in the salt. Blend in the flour thoroughly.
- Whip the egg whites until they form stiff peaks, then fold them into the batter.
- Dust the shrimp lightly with flour, then dip them into the batter. Allow any excess batter to drip off.
- Carefully place the shrimp, 4 at a time, in the hot oil. Fry until golden brown. As each batch is finished, drain on absorbent paper, then place in the oven to keep warm. Repeat until all the shrimp have been fried.
- Serve 4 shrimp per person, accompanied by the coulis and garnished with the flat leaf parsley.

Wine recommendation: Riesling, champagne, or sparkling chardonnay

Oyster and Spinach Strudel

Four to Six Servings

FOR THE FILLING

3 tablespoons dry white wine
8 large fresh oysters, cut into ¼-inch pieces
8 ounces fresh spinach, well washed and dried, stems trimmed

4 tablespoons (½ stick) unsalted butter
salt and pepper as needed
2 tablespoons butter
1½ tablespoons flour
½ cup milk

FOR THE PASTRY

1 package frozen phyllo dough

½ cup melted butter

TO PREPARE THE FILLING
- Bring the wine and oysters to a boil, and simmer for 1 minute. Drain, discarding the liquid, and set the oysters aside.
- Sauté the spinach in the butter for 3 minutes. Season with salt and pepper. When cool, chop into approximately ¼-inch pieces.
- Cook the butter and flour together in a pan for 5 minutes over low heat. Do not brown. Blend in the milk thoroughly. Simmer 5 minutes, stirring until the sauce is very thick and smooth. Set aside.

Coulis, *a French term for a type of sauce, was first mentioned in print in* Le Cuisinier François, *written in 1651, by François-Pierre de la Varenne, cook to Henri IV. Technically, a coulis consisted of the naturally occurring juices that a roast releases during cooking. From such pan juices were created many sauces, some thickened with starch, some not.*

In contemporary culinary parlance, a coulis is a light sauce thickened by a puree of its ingredients.

Strudel is a dish native to Austria, Germany, and central Europe in general. It has been called the national dish of Bavaria and is found with fillings both savory and sweet, made of ingredients as diverse as apples, raisins, cherries, nuts, cabbage, cheese, and vegetables.

A strudel dough is made of flour, egg, oil or lard, and salt and is stretched carefully by hand. The high fat content, plus a high-gluten flour creates a dough elastic enough to stretch paper-thin. However, given the intensive labor required to make strudel dough from scratch, as well as its level of difficulty (the dough often breaks during stretching), it is perfectly acceptable to substitute phyllo, or filo, a high-quality manufactured dough imported from Greece, which is available frozen in most supermarkets.

The Bavarian style of strudel is generally a long cylindrical shape, but American cooks have adapted other styles of wrapping. The triangular shape presented in this recipe is Middle Eastern in origin.

Cut the phyllo dough sheets lengthwise into 4 strips (*A*). Fold a corner of each strip over the filling (*B*). Fold the first triangle up along the strip (*C*). Brush the triangle with melted butter (*D*).

TO PREPARE THE PASTRY

- Preheat an oven to 350° F.
- Brush a sheet of phyllo lightly with melted butter. Place another sheet on top, and brush with butter. Repeat these steps until there are 6 layers of buttered phyllo. Cut it lengthwise into 4 strips, approximately 2½ inches wide.
- Blend the oysters, spinach, and sauce together thoroughly in a bowl. The mixture should be fairly dry and firm.
- Place a heaping teaspoon of the filling a couple of inches from one end of a phyllo strip. Fold one corner of the dough triangularly over the filling. Continue folding this triangle all the way to the end of the strip (see diagram). Brush with melted butter. Repeat until all the filling is used, preparing more phyllo strips as needed. This recipe should yield 20 to 24 individual strudels.

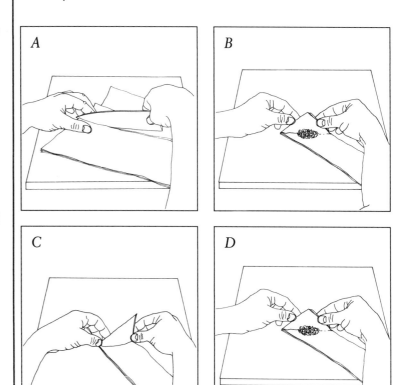

- Transfer the strudels to a lightly buttered baking sheet. Bake for 4 to 6 minutes, or until golden brown.

Wine recommendation: very dry, very crisp chardonnay or fumé blanc

SOUPS

Chilled Garden Vegetable Soup with Purple Basil

Four Servings

2 pounds ripe tomatoes,
   peeled and cored
1 large European cucumber,
   roughly chopped, except
   for ¼ cup fine julienne
1 small Spanish onion,
   peeled and roughly
   chopped
1 yellow bell pepper, seeded
   and roughly chopped,
   except for ¼ cup fine
   julienne

1 garlic clove, minced
½ cup fresh white bread
   crumbs
¼ cup red wine vinegar
1 cup chicken stock
leaves of 3 sprigs fresh
   oregano
½ bunch fresh purple basil
   leaves
salt and pepper as needed

- Place all of the ingredients except for 4 basil leaves and the julienned cucumber and bell pepper into a food processor. Puree. Pour into a container, cover, and refrigerate for 24 hours.
- Season the soup to taste with salt and pepper, ladle into 4 individual serving bowls, and top each serving with a purple basil leaf and some julienned cucumber and yellow pepper.

Paradise Soup

Four Servings

3 large ripe tomatoes,
   peeled and cored
¼ small Spanish onion
juice and zest of 1 lemon
pinch salt
pinch pepper
¾ cup sour cream
12 melon balls (seasonal
   variety)

1 Granny Smith apple,
   peeled, cored, and cut
   into fine julienne
½ cup peeled and finely
   julienned cucumber
8 mint leaves

Botanically speaking, a fruit is a ripened ovary containing one or more seeds of a plant. By this definition, tomatoes, cucumbers, green beans, eggplants, pepper, pea pods, corn, nuts, avocados, pumpkins, squashes, okra, and olives are all fruit. This technical definition is not generally respected, however, and these are usually considered vegetables. Indeed, in the late nineteenth century, the U.S. Supreme Court officially ruled that the tomato is a vegetable, the impetus for the decision being that, at the time, import duty was charged on vegetables, but not on fruits.

- Puree the tomatoes, onion, lemon juice and zest, salt, and pepper in a blender or food processor. Pour into a mixing bowl, and blend in ½ cup of the sour cream. Cover, and refrigerate for at least 4 hours.
- In each of 4 large chilled soup bowls, place 3 melon balls. Divide the soup among the 4 bowls, and top with the remaining sour cream. Sprinkle with julienned apple and cucumber, and garnish each serving with 2 mint leaves.

Cream of Asparagus Soup

Four Servings

½ pound very fat asparagus
2½ tablespoons unsalted
  butter
1 small Spanish onion,
  minced
1 bay leaf
pinch nutmeg
⅓ cup flour

2 cups hot milk
1 cup hot white stock (veal
  or chicken)
¼ cup heavy cream
salt and pepper as needed
1 tablespoon chopped
  chervil

- Trim the asparagus to 6-inch lengths, and discard the woody ends. Peel the stalks, reserving the peel, and cut them in half. Cut the bottom halves into ⅛-inch pieces, combine these with the peelings, and set aside. Slant cut the top halves into ¼-inch pieces, and set these aside.
- In a heavy-gauge soup pot, melt the butter over a medium fire. Sauté the onion, bay leaf, and reserved asparagus peelings and pieces for about 5 minutes.
- Add the nutmeg and flour, and blend well. Cook for about 5 minutes, stirring frequently.
- Stir the hot milk thoroughly into the flour mixture. Bring to a boil, add the hot stock, and stir well.
- Let the soup simmer about 15 minutes, stirring occasionally.
- Blanch the remaining asparagus pieces in ¼ cup of lightly salted water until they are tender but still firm. Drain, adding the blanching liquid to the simmering soup.
- Carefully puree the hot soup in a blender or food processor. (Be very cautious: puree only a small amount at a time, holding the top of the blender or processor firmly in place.)
- Strain the pureed soup through a fine sieve, and return it to the soup pot. Bring it back to a simmer, then stir in the

heavy cream and blanched asparagus pieces. Season to taste with salt and pepper, sprinkle on the chopped chervil, and serve.

Corn Chowder

Four to Six Servings

4 slices bacon, cut into ¼-inch dice	1½ cups ¼-inch-diced red potatoes
2 tablespoons butter	3 cups chicken stock
1 small Spanish onion, cut into ¼-inch dice	1 cup half-and-half or light cream
1 stalk celery, cut into ¼-inch dice	1 tablespoon Worcestershire sauce
1½ cups whole-kernel corn	salt and pepper to taste

- In a large soup pot, sauté the bacon until golden brown and crisp. Pour off the fat, and discard.
- Add the butter, onion, and celery, and sauté 5 minutes.
- Stir in the corn and potatoes.
- Add the chicken stock, and simmer until the potatoes are tender, approximately 30 minutes.
- Puree ½ of this mixture in a blender or food processor, return to the soup pot, and bring the soup back to a simmer. Add the cream and Worcestershire sauce, and bring to a boil. Season to taste with salt and pepper.

SALADS

The Tower Restaurant, world headquarters of ARA Services, is located in the ARA Tower building, 1101 Market Street, Philadelphia, Pennsylvania.

Tower Garden Salad

Four Servings

FOR THE SAUCE

1 red bell pepper, cut into eighths and simmered in boiling salted water until tender
¼ cup hazelnut or walnut oil
¼ cup olive oil

1 shallot, chopped
1 garlic clove, chopped
¼ cup white wine vinegar
1 tablespoon Dijon mustard
¼ teaspoon salt
¼ teaspoon white pepper

FOR THE SALAD

1 small head Boston lettuce
1 small head radicchio
½ bunch fresh spinach leaves, stems removed
1 bunch watercress, stems removed

12 mushrooms, sliced
6 fat radishes, sliced paper-thin
1 tablespoon minced fresh chives

TO PREPARE THE SAUCE

• Puree all the ingredients in a blender or food processor. Adjust seasoning.

TO PREPARE THE SALAD

• Tear all of the salad greens into bite-size pieces, rinse well in cold water, and spin or pat dry. Refrigerate until ready to serve.
• Place the salad greens in a salad bowl. Toss with an appropriate quantity of the sauce. Arrange on chilled salad plates, and top with the sliced mushrooms, sliced radishes, and chopped chives.

Atwater Salad

Four Servings

Atwater's is a public restaurant located on the thirtieth floor of the US Bancorp building at 111 S.W. Fifth Avenue, Portland, Oregon. For dinner and Sunday brunch reservations, telephone (503) 275-3600.

FOR THE VINAIGRETTE
½ cup grated fresh ginger root
1 tablespoon dry mustard
2 tablespoons lemon juice
1 teaspoon granulated sugar
2 tablespoons tarragon vinegar

1 cup olive oil
1 small shallot, minced
1 small garlic clove, minced
pinch salt
pinch pepper

FOR THE SALAD
1 head butter lettuce
1 small head red leaf lettuce
1 small head radicchio
1 ripe avocado, peeled, pitted, and cut into 4 wedges

4 ripe cherry tomatoes
½ pound cooked bay (titi) shrimp

TO PREPARE THE VINAIGRETTE
- Wrap the grated ginger in cheesecloth, and squeeze the juice into a blender. Discard the pulp.
- Add the remaining ingredients to the ginger juice, and puree. Set aside.

TO PREPARE THE SALAD
- Tear the lettuces into bite-size pieces, rinse well in cold water, and spin or pat dry. Refrigerate until ready to serve.
- Make lengthwise, ¼-inch-wide, parallel cuts in each avocado quarter, beginning ½ inch from one end. Press down and to one side on each quarter, creating a fan. Transfer each fan to an individual serving plate, and place a cherry tomato next to each one.
- Toss the salad greens with the vinaigrette, and divide among the 4 plates. Top with the bay shrimp, and serve.

Fennel and Cucumber Salad

Four Servings

⅓ cup olive oil
2 tablespoons rice wine
   vinegar
pinch salt
pinch granulated sugar
1 fennel root, sliced very
   thin
⅓ European cucumber,
   peeled, split lengthwise,
   and sliced very thin

8 large radishes, sliced very
   thin
1 small Bermuda onion,
   sliced very thin
1 bunch fresh chives,
   minced
2 ripe tomatoes, cut into 12
   wedges each
freshly ground black pepper
   as needed

- Blend the oil, vinegar, salt, and sugar in a mixing bowl until the salt and sugar are dissolved. Add all of the vegetables (except the tomatoes) and half of the chives. Toss, and arrange on 4 individual chilled salad plates. Garnish each plate with 6 tomato wedges, and sprinkle with the remaining chopped chives and some pepper.

Wine recommendation: dry Riesling

Main Courses

FISH

Halibut with Yellow Pepper Sauce and Chive Flowers

Four Servings

FOR THE SAUCE

2 yellow bell peppers, cut
  into 8 pieces each
1 shallot, minced
1 garlic clove, minced
½ teaspoon fresh thyme
  leaves

3 tablespoons olive oil
1 cup fish stock or clam
  juice
pinch salt
pinch white pepper

FOR THE HALIBUT

4 5- to 6-ounce halibut
  fillets, skinned
juice of 1 small lemon

salt and pepper as needed
1 shallot, minced
8 purple chive flowers

TO PREPARE THE SAUCE

- Sauté the pepper, shallot, garlic, and thyme in the olive oil until the pepper is tender. Add the stock, salt, and pepper. Cook for a few minutes more, then puree in a blender or food processor. Return to the pan, and keep warm until ready to serve.

TO PREPARE THE HALIBUT

- Preheat an oven to 375° F. Butter an ovenproof casserole or baking dish.
- Place the fillets in the buttered dish, pour the lemon juice over them, and sprinkle with the salt, pepper, and shallots.

Our colonial ancestors used wildflowers in their cooking, a practice that has come back into vogue recently. Edible flowers can be used in a variety of dishes, particularly in, but not limited to, salads. Many varieties are UNSAFE to consume, either because they are naturally poisonous, like the azalea, daffodil, oleander, poinsettia, wisteria, and others, or because they have been sprayed with insecticides. The safest edible flowers are those you raise at home. They should be picked early in the morning on the day they are to be consumed, gently rinsed, wrapped loosely in paper towels, then stored in plastic bags in the refrigerator until they are to be used.

Apple blossoms, light pink and white, have a fresh fragrance and slightly floral taste. Before you try them, make sure that the trees were not sprayed. In Japan and China, people believe that eating the chrysanthemum increases longevity, makes teeth grow again, and turns white hair black. Aromatic and crisp, they enhance chicken, egg, shrimp, or salad dishes. Marigolds add a rich color to soups, stews, sauces, and puddings. Some say their taste is similar to saffron. Nasturtiums, spicy and peppery, spark up both the taste and, with their bright hues, the look of salads (especially potato). Nasturtium vegetable soup was a favorite of President Eisenhower's, perhaps in part because the flowers contain an herbal type of penicillin and a lot of Vitamin C. Pansy centers taste a bit like root beer or cinnamon and make an excellent, colorful garnish pressed onto an iced cake. In France, pansy oil is still rubbed on eyelids to induce love at first sight. Tulips, stripped of their pollen and stigma, can be used as a garnish or stuffed with herbed cheese to serve as an appetizer. Violet stems and leaves are edible, but the blossoms are consumed the most. Most familiar in candied form, they are used to garnish desserts and also make an excellent flavoring for syrup, ice cream, or whipped cream. Medieval philosopher Albertus Magnus wrote that gathering violets during the final quarter of the moon would cause all one's wishes to come true.

Cover, and bake for 8 to 10 minutes, or until the fish is tender.
- For each serving, ladle about ¼ cup of sauce onto a serving plate. Place a fish fillet on top of the sauce, and garnish with 2 chive flowers.

Wine recommendation: rich chardonnay

Poached Salmon, Tarragon Butter Sauce

Four Servings

FOR THE SALMON

1 cup ⅛-inch-julienned carrots	1 bay leaf
1 cup ⅛-inch-julienned leeks	8 black peppercorns
4 cups fish stock or water	1 cup dry white wine
juice of 1 lemon	4 6-ounce Alaskan salmon fillets
¼ teaspoon salt	
1 small Spanish onion, peeled and cut into quarters	

FOR THE SAUCE

¼ cup dry white wine	2 tablespoons chopped fresh tarragon leaves
juice of 1 lemon	
8 tablespoons (1 stick) unsalted butter, cut into ½-inch cubes	

TO PREPARE THE SALMON
- Simmer the carrots and leeks in boiling salted water until tender but still firm. Drain and set aside.
- Combine all the remaining ingredients, except the salmon, and bring them to a simmer.
- Place the salmon fillets in the poaching medium, and simmer them *very gently*. After 5 minutes, turn off the fire.

TO PREPARE THE SAUCE
- Bring the wine and the lemon juice to a boil, and simmer until reduced by half.
- Over low heat, add the butter, and stir continuously until it is fully emulsified. Add the tarragon leaves, then remove the sauce from the fire.

- Using a slotted spatula, remove the salmon fillets from the poaching liquid, and drain them on absorbent paper. Place them on a warmed serving plate, and top them with the blanched carrots and leeks, then the butter sauce.

Wine recommendation: rich chardonnay

Roast Salmon with Seasonal Vegetable Medley

Four Servings

FOR THE SAUCE

1 slice fresh white bread, crusts trimmed	1 cup chopped fresh parsley
4 tablespoons heavy cream	½ teaspoon salt
2 garlic cloves	¼ teaspoon cayenne pepper
leaves of 4 sprigs fresh thyme	4 tablespoons (½ stick) butter
leaves of 4 sprigs fresh marjoram	¼ cup olive oil

FOR THE SALMON

4 ¼-inch-thick slices slab bacon	6 stalks medium-thick asparagus, peeled and cut into ¼-inch dice
1 medium Spanish onion, peeled and cut into ¼-inch dice	¼ fennel root, peeled and cut into ¼-inch dice
1 small white turnip, peeled and cut into ¼-inch dice	2 cups fish stock
1 medium carrot, peeled and cut into ¼-inch dice	4 7- to 8-ounce Chinook salmon fillets
1 parsnip, peeled and cut into ¼-inch dice	salt and pepper as needed

TO PREPARE THE SAUCE
- Puree all of the sauce ingredients in a blender.

TO PREPARE THE SALMON
- Preheat an oven to 350° F.
- Fry the bacon in a large cast-iron skillet or sauté pan until it is golden brown and very crisp. Reserving the fat, remove the bacon, and drain on absorbent paper.
- Sauté the onion for 5 minutes. Add the remaining vegetables, and sauté over a low flame for 3 more minutes.

Salmon is an anadromous fish, meaning that it lives in salt water but returns to its natal freshwater streams or rivers to spawn. Once found in great abundance from the Hudson River and up the New England coast to Canada, today, it is found only in certain rivers in Maine and Canada, a victim of our polluted waters.

Most of the remaining salmon beds of North America are found on the Pacific coast, between northern California and Alaska. But, even there, numbers are diminishing as a result of pollution, deep-sea overfishing, and damming (salmon cannot return to their spawning grounds unless a river dam is equipped with a special fish ladder).

Salmon season runs from May to December, and varieties include Chinook or King (the largest variety—the record catch is over one hundred pounds and the average is fifteen to eighty pounds), Red or Sockeye (which has dark red flesh, is rich in oil, and averages twelve pounds), Coho or Silver (which has orange flesh and weighs in at four to twelve pounds), Pink or Humpback (which matures the fastest—in two years— and reaches a maximum weight of eight pounds), and Chum or Keta (an eight- to sixteen-pound fish whose pale flesh is valued little but whose roe is prized).

If asparagus is not available, you can substitute any other variety of fresh green vegetable—broccoli, string beans, zucchini, etc.

- Add the fish stock, and bring to a simmer.
- Season the salmon fillets with salt and pepper, and place them in the pan. Cover, and place in the oven for 8 to 10 minutes.
- Gently remove the salmon fillets to a platter, and set aside, keeping warm.
- Place the pan with the vegetables on the stove, and simmer vigorously until the liquid is reduced by half.
- Stir 4 tablespoons of the savory herb sauce into the vegetables, and remove from the fire.
- Place the salmon fillets on serving plates, and top with the vegetable-sauce mix. Serve with steamed baby red potatoes and any remaining sauce.

Wine recommendation: rich chardonnay

Grilled Ling Cod, Orange-Lime Salsa

If ling cod is unavailable, you may wish to substitute red snapper.

Four Servings

FOR THE SALSA

5 oranges	½ cup minced Bermuda
5 limes	onion
1 tablespoon chopped fresh cilantro	½ jalapeño pepper, minced
	juice of 1 lemon

FOR THE COD

4 5- to 6-ounce ling cod fillets	salt, pepper, and olive oil as needed

TO PREPARE THE SALSA
- Pare the oranges and limes with a sharp knife, making sure to remove all the pith. Holding the fruit over a small bowl (to catch the juice), remove the fruit segments by cutting on either side of the skin that separates them.
- Remove any seeds from the segments, add the fruit to the bowl, then squeeze the juice from the remaining pulp into the same bowl. Add the cilantro, onion, lemon juice, and jalapeño pepper.

TO PREPARE THE COD
- Prepare an outdoor grill.
- Sprinkle the fillets lightly with salt and pepper, and coat lightly with oil. Grill for 4 to 5 minutes on each side, brush-

ing with some of the salsa juice while they cook. Serve with a side of the salsa and corn on the cob.

Wine recommendation: spicy Riesling

Charred Tuna, Olive Paste

Four Servings

FOR THE PASTE
1 cup pitted dried black olives
2 garlic cloves

1 anchovy fillet
3 tablespoons olive oil

FOR THE SAUCE
¼ cup dry white wine
3 tablespoons rice wine vinegar
¼ teaspoon minced shallot
¼ teaspoon minced garlic

¼ cup heavy cream
16 tablespoons (2 sticks) unsalted butter
salt and pepper as needed

FOR THE TUNA
4 5-ounce fresh tuna steaks
salt, pepper, and sesame oil as needed

4 ounces (2 cups) fresh spinach, stemmed, well rinsed

FOR SERVING
¼ cup ¼-inch-diced red bell pepper

¼ cup ¼-inch-diced yellow bell pepper

TO PREPARE THE PASTE
• Puree all the ingredients in a food processor. Cover, and refrigerate until ready to serve.

TO PREPARE THE SAUCE
• Place the wine, vinegar, shallot, and garlic in a small saucepan. Bring to a simmer, and reduce until almost completely dry. Add the cream, and bring to a simmer. Add the butter, 2 tablespoons at a time, stirring continuously until it is completely incorporated. Strain, season to taste with salt and pepper, and keep warm until ready to serve.

Botanically a fruit but considered a vegetable in culinary applications, olives are native to the eastern Mediterranean and were cultivated as early as 3500 B.C. They are about 18 percent oil by weight, and this oil has been used not only in cooking but for fuel and in cosmetics. Today, however, 90 percent of the world's olive production is used to make cooking oil.

Spanish explorers brought the olive to the New World in the fifteenth century, where it was cultivated in Mexico in the seventeenth and eighteenth centuries. Franciscan monks planted olive tree cuttings in California as they established missions along their "Mission Trail." Still, roughly 98 percent of the world's olive acreage remains in the Mediterranean, although California, whose inland central valley possesses a similar climate, is also a major grower.

Raw olives are incredibly bitter and so must be cured before being eaten. Since ancient Roman times, this has been accomplished by first soaking the fruit in a lye solution, then vigorously washing them. Today's Greek olives are packed in salt, then brined; green olives are picked before they ripen, treated with lye, and brined; and California olives are first dipped in a solution of ferrous gluconate—organic iron salt—to fix their color, then treated with lye, and finally brined.

TO PREPARE THE TUNA

- Season the tuna steaks lightly with salt and pepper. Brush lightly with sesame oil.
- Heat a nonstick pan over a high flame. When the pan is very hot, sear the steaks for 1 minute on each side. Remove, and set aside, keeping warm. Wipe out the pan, and return it to a medium flame.
- Add about a teaspoon of sesame oil to the pan, then the spinach, and sauté for 2 minutes. Season with salt and pepper.

TO SERVE

- Slice the tuna steaks into ¼-inch slices. Ladle ¼ cup of sauce on each of 4 serving plates. Place one-quarter of the spinach on each plate, and sprinkle it with the diced peppers. Arrange the sliced tuna in a fan on the spinach, and garnish with two dollops of the olive paste.

Wine recommendation: Pinot Noir

Alder-planked Salmon, Olympia Oysters

Four Servings

20 Olympia oysters	1 cup dry white wine
2 medium bulbs of fennel root, washed, trimmed, and sliced ¼-inch thick	2 cups crème fraîche
	4 6-ounce salmon fillets or steaks, skin on
3 tablespoons butter	salt, pepper, and vegetable oil as needed
1 shallot, minced	
2 tablespoons Pernod	

- Preheat an oven to 400° F.
- Rub a well-seasoned plank of alder with vegetable oil, and place it in the oven for 1 hour. The wood should be brown and smoking.
- Place the oysters on the board, and roast them for 5 minutes or so, until they pop. Remove them from their shells, place them in a small bowl, and set aside.
- Reduce the oven temperature to 350° F, wipe the board clean, and return it to the oven.
- Sauté the fennel in the butter for 3 or 4 minutes. Add the shallot, sauté several minutes more, then add the Pernod and wine, and reduce until almost completely dry. Blend

Only prepare this recipe in a well-ventilated kitchen—once the board is placed in the oven, it will begin to smoke.

The native tribes who inhabited the coastal areas of the Pacific Northwest transformed native varieties of fish into a dry, hard jerky by smoking them with green alder branches. Ubiquitous in coastal plains and stream beds, alder burns slowly and produces considerable smoke, making it ideal for smoking and preserving. Bill Geary first experimented with using alder at Atwater's by strapping fish fillets to alderwood planks then placing them in a rotisserie. George Poston, his successor at the restaurant, further refined the technique.

in the crème fraîche, bring to a simmer, and remove from the fire. Keep warm until ready to serve.
- Sprinkle the salmon fillets lightly with salt and pepper, then brush them lightly with oil. Place them on the smoking hot plank, and roast for 8 minutes.
- Add the oysters to the fennel, and warm briefly. Spoon some of the fennel and oysters onto 4 serving plates, and top each serving with a salmon fillet.

Wine recommendation: rich, dry chardonnay

SHELLFISH

Seafood Brochettes with Grilled Leeks

Four Servings

8 large sea scallops
8 spot prawns, peeled and deveined
4 medium leeks
2 or 3 razor clams, shucked and cut into 8 1-inch pieces each
2 garlic cloves, minced
1 shallot, minced

8 tablespoons (1 stick) butter
½ cup olive oil
½ cup chopped assorted fresh herbs (chervil, parsley, basil, tarragon, and/or marjoram)
juice of 1 lemon
salt and pepper as needed

- Prepare an outdoor grill.
- Cut the roots and about half of the dark green tops from the leeks. The remaining leeks should be about 8 inches long.
- Split the leeks in half lengthwise. Rinse them *very well* in cold water, removing any sand and soil caught between the leaves.
- Cook the leeks in boiling salted water for 5 minutes. Remove, and plunge into cold water. Drain, pat dry, and set aside.
- Spear the shellfish on 4 10-inch skewers, alternating the 3 varieties. Set aside.
- Sauté the garlic and shallots in the butter and olive oil for

Spot prawns, also known as raccoon or broken-back shrimp, are found on the West Coast from California to Alaska. Although they come in all sizes, 16/20s would be best for this dish. If spot prawns are not available, standard Gulf of Mexico shrimp can be substituted.

Start an outdoor grill with standard charcoal briquets and an odorless starter fluid. Allow a half hour for the fire to peak, then another half hour for its heat to diminish slightly. At this point, the coals will produce an even heat and will tend not to flame up during grilling.

About twenty minutes before you are ready to start grilling, place some aromatic wood on top of the briquets. You might try alderwood, hickory, or even grapevine cuttings. Packaged wood chips are often available at hardware and garden shops.

4 or 5 minutes. Add the herbs, lemon juice, and salt and pepper to taste.
- Brush the brochettes and leeks liberally with the butter and-herb mixture. Grill for 4 to 5 minutes on each side. The seafood should be firm to the touch but still moist inside, and the leeks should be golden brown. Serve with rice pilaf and a garden salad.

Wine recommendation: Pinot Noir

Cioppino is a fish stew unique to northern California, made with Dungeness crab and a tomato sauce base. While its name clearly derives from the Italian ciuppin, *Genoa's name for its pureed fish soup, it has much more in common with Leghorn's* cacciucco *or even Marseilles's* bouillabaisse.

Monterey Bay Cioppino

Four to Six Servings

2 shallots, roughly chopped
4 large garlic cloves, roughly chopped
1 green bell pepper, cut into ½-inch dice
1 red bell pepper, cut into ½-inch dice
4 tablespoons olive oil
2 large ripe tomatoes, peeled and roughly chopped
2 tablespoons tomato paste
½ teaspoon minced fresh oregano leaves
1 tablespoon minced fresh basil
3 tablespoons minced fresh parsley

¼ teaspoon salt
¼ teaspoon freshly ground pepper
2 live Dungeness crabs, cleaned and cut into 1-inch pieces
2 pounds fresh mussels, cleaned and debearded
½ pound 16/20 count prawns, unshelled
4 cups dry white wine
6 ounces sea bass fillet, cut into 1-by-½-inch pieces
6 ounces halibut fillet, cut into 1-by-½-inch pieces
6 ounces fresh sea scallops

- In a very large pan, sauté the shallots, garlic, and peppers in the olive oil, covered, for 6 minutes. Blend in the to-matoes, tomato paste, salt, and pepper, then the chopped oregano, basil, and half of the parsley. Add the crab, mus-sels, and prawns. Pour the wine over this, cover, and simmer 5 minutes.
- Add the sea bass and halibut, cover, and simmer 5 minutes more. Finally, stir in the scallops, cover, and remove from the fire.
- Allow the cioppino to sit for 5 minutes before serving, then

ladle it into large soup bowls, and top with the remaining parsley.

Wine recommendation: Pinot Noir

Lobster Ragout, Provence Style

Four Servings

FOR THE RAGOUT

juice of 2 lemons
1 tablespoon salt
4 sprigs fresh dill
4 live 1¼-pound lobsters
1½ cups select button
   mushrooms, sliced
4 tablespoons olive oil
2 large garlic cloves, minced

8 ripe plum tomatoes,
   peeled and cut ½-inch
   dice
½ cup dry white wine
4 dashes Tabasco sauce
salt and pepper to taste
2 tablespoons butter

FOR THE PASTA

2 tablespoons olive oil
1 tablespoon salt
1 pound fresh fettucine

1 tablespoon butter
¼ cup chopped fresh
   parsley

FOR SERVING

freshly grated Parmesan
   cheese as needed

TO PREPARE THE RAGOUT

- In a large pot, bring 2 gallons of water to a boil with the lemon juice, salt, and dill. Add the lobsters, and boil for 10 minutes. Remove, and plunge them into cold water.
- When the lobsters have cooled, remove them from the water, and crack their tails and claws. Remove the meat, discarding the shells. Cut the meat in ¼-inch slices, and set aside.
- Sauté the mushrooms in hot olive oil until they are golden brown.
- Add the garlic and tomatoes, simmer for 3 minutes, then add the white wine, Tabasco, salt, and pepper.
- Add the lobster meat, bring the mixture to a boil, then stir in the butter. When the butter is completely emulsified, remove the ragout from the fire, and set it aside.

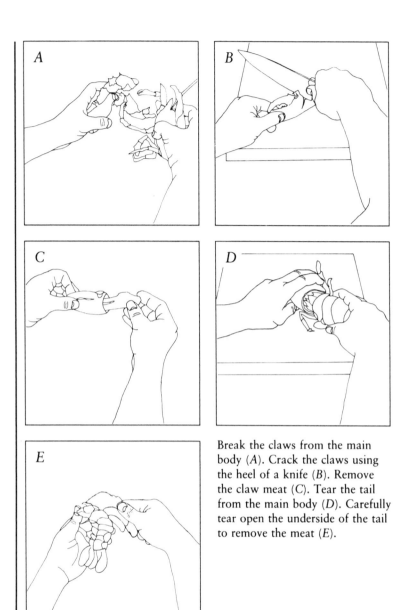

Break the claws from the main body (A). Crack the claws using the heel of a knife (B). Remove the claw meat (C). Tear the tail from the main body (D). Carefully tear open the underside of the tail to remove the meat (E).

TO PREPARE THE PASTA
- Bring 1 gallon of water, the olive oil, and the salt to a rolling boil. Add the fettucine. Return the water to a boil, and cook the pasta about 1 minute, or until it is tender but al dente. Drain, and return it to the pot. Add the butter and chopped parsley.

TO SERVE
- Arrange the pasta in 4 large soup plates or an appropriate serving plate. Spoon on some warm ragout, and top with grated Parmesan cheese.

Wine recommendation: Beaujolais or Grenache

Scallops Méditerranée

Four Servings

1 pound bay or sea scallops
2 tablespoons unsalted
   butter
1 shallot, minced
¼ cup dry white wine
pinch saffron
1 cup heavy cream

6 fresh basil leaves, cut into
   fine julienne
1 ripe medium tomato,
   peeled, seeded, and cut
   into fine julienne
salt and pepper as needed

- Sauté the scallops in the butter for 1 minute on each side over a medium flame. Remove with a slotted or perforated spoon, and set aside.
- Sauté the shallot in the same pan for 2 minutes. Add the white wine and saffron, and simmer until almost completely dry. Add the cream, and simmer until reduced by half. Add the basil, tomato, and scallops, and simmer another minute. Season to taste with salt and pepper.

Wine recommendation: rich sauvignon blanc

POULTRY

Sautéed Baby Chickens
with Shiitakes and Ginger

Four Servings

12 medium shiitake
   mushrooms, stems
   removed
4 12-ounce baby chickens
   (*poussins*), split along the
   back, breast bones
   removed
salt and pepper as needed

1 tablespoon unsalted butter
2 garlic cloves, minced
1 tablespoon very finely
   julienned fresh ginger
   root
1½ cups chicken stock
1 tablespoon soy sauce

- Preheat an oven to 400° F. Arrange the mushroom caps in groups of 3 in a roasting pan.
- Season the chickens lightly with salt and pepper, then sauté in the butter, skin side down, until lightly browned.
- Place a chicken, skin side up, on each of the sets of mushroom caps in the roasting pan, and rub the top surface of each with garlic and ginger. Roast for 10 to 12 minutes.
- Place the roasting pan on top of the stove, and add the stock and soy sauce. Simmer for 2 minutes.
- Serve 1 chicken per person, with 3 shiitake mushrooms and some of the broth spooned over.

Wine recommendation: light zinfandel

Grilled Breast of Chicken, Seasonal Herbs

Four Servings

4 6- to 8-ounce boneless chicken breasts, pounded lightly	1 teaspoon fresh thyme leaves
salt and pepper as needed	1 teaspoon fresh rosemary leaves
juice of 1 lemon	2 cups chicken stock
1 tablespoon Worcestershire sauce	4 tablespoons (½ stick) unsalted butter, cut into ½-inch cubes
1 cup dry white wine	
2 tablespoons chopped fresh basil	2 tablespoons chopped fresh chives

- Sprinkle the chicken breasts lightly with salt and pepper. Place in a bowl with the lemon juice, Worcestershire sauce, white wine, basil, thyme, and rosemary. Mix together well, cover, and refrigerate for 2 hours.
- Prepare an outdoor grill.
- Remove the breasts from the marinade, and drain them. Place the marinade in a saucepan with the chicken stock. Simmer until the liquid is reduced by two-thirds.
- Place the breasts on the grill, skin side down, and grill until golden brown. Turn over, and finish cooking. Remove to a platter, keeping them warm.
- Add the butter to the reduced marinade, stirring continuously until it is fully incorporated. Season the sauce to taste with salt and pepper. Strain.

There is nothing quite as savory as meat, poultry, fish, or vegetables grilled over an open fire. In recent years, mesquite charcoal, usually imported from Mexico, has come into vogue, but many other woods also can add flavor.

The grill fire can be started with ordinary charcoal briquets, using an odorless liquid starter, or with the self-starting variety. Allow the fire to burn for 30 minutes, then lay some aromatic wood on it —perhaps alderwood, hickory, grapevine cuttings, or fresh herb stems. (Packaged wood chips are often available at hardware or garden shops.) Allow the aromatic wood to burn for 20 minutes, then begin grilling.

- Place each chicken breast skin side up on an appropriate serving plate. Top with sauce, and sprinkle with chopped chives.

Wine recommendation: merlot or rich, strong chardonnay

Petaluma Breast of Duck

Four Servings

Petaluma is a town approximately thirty miles north of San Francisco, known for its exceptionally fine poultry.

FOR THE MOUSSE

10 ounces veal sweetbreads	½ teaspoon salt
¼ cup cognac	½ teaspoon white pepper
¼ cup dry vermouth	1 teaspoon lemon juice
2 tablespoons chopped fresh basil	2 large egg whites
	1 cup heavy cream

FOR THE DUCK

4 duck breast halves, skinned and boned	½ cup fresh whole raspberries
3 tablespoons butter	2 tablespoons prepared horseradish
2 tablespoons minced shallot	1½ cups heavy cream
½ cup dry vermouth	salt and pepper as needed

TO PREPARE THE MOUSSE
- Trim the sweetbreads of excess skin. Cut into roughly 1-inch pieces, and place in a bowl.
- Add the cognac, vermouth, and basil. Cover, and marinate 3 hours.
- Drain the sweetbreads, discarding the marinade. Puree in a food processor along with the salt, pepper, lemon juice, egg whites, and cream. Remove to a small bowl. Cover, and refrigerate for 1 hour.

TO PREPARE THE DUCK
- Preheat an oven to 350° F.
- Butterfly each duck breast by carefully slicing it in half horizontally to within a half-inch of one side.
- Spread each opened breast half with a layer of the mousse, leaving a ½-inch border clear of filling.
- Roll up each breast half lengthwise, then tie with cotton cord or butcher's twine.

- Melt 1 tablespoon of the butter in a cast-iron skillet, lightly brown the rolled breast halves, then place the skillet in the oven, and roast for 20 minutes.
- Remove the breast halves from the skillet, and set them aside in a warm place. Place the skillet over a medium flame, melt the remaining butter, and sauté the shallots for several minutes. Deglaze the skillet with the vermouth. Add the raspberries and horseradish, and simmer until reduced by half. Add the cream, and reduce once again by half. Puree in a food processor or blender, and strain through a fine sieve. Return the sauce to the pan, bring it to a simmer, and season to taste with salt and pepper.
- Remove the cord from the breast halves, and slice each one on the bias into 4 pieces. Place about ¼ cup of sauce on each of 4 serving plates, and arrange 4 pieces of duck on top. Serve with spinach linguine.

Wine recommendation: Pinot Noir

The more than six dozen varieties of domesticated duck found worldwide are all believed to have descended from the mallard, which is native to Europe, Asia, North Africa, and North America.

Breast of Duck with Raspberry and Tangerine

Four Servings

FOR THE DUCK

1 tablespoon cracked black pepper	4 boneless duck breasts, skin on
½ teaspoon salt	3 cups dry vermouth

FOR THE SAUCE

1 tablespoon butter	salt and pepper as needed
2 large shallots, minced	3 tangerines, peeled, seeded, and trimmed of pith and membranes
3¼ cups fresh raspberries	
juice of 2 tangerines	
1 cup demi-glace	
2 tablespoons unsalted butter	

FOR SERVING
1 bunch fresh watercress

TO PREPARE THE DUCK
- Rub the salt and cracked pepper into the duck breasts. Place in a bowl, and add the vermouth. Cover, refrigerate, and marinate for 24 hours.

- Preheat an oven to the lowest setting possible.
- Place a cast-iron skillet or sauté pan over a medium flame, and allow it to become very hot. Remove the breasts from the vermouth, reserving the marinade, and pat them dry. Carefully place them in the skillet, skin side down, and cook over medium heat for 5 minutes, or until the skin is a very dark brown. Turn them over, and cook for 30 to 60 seconds more. Remove them to a platter, and place in the oven to stay warm.

TO PREPARE THE SAUCE
- Pour any excess fat from the skillet, and add the butter. When it is melted, sauté the shallots for approximately 3 minutes. Add 2 cups of the raspberries, and mash them into the shallots. Add the tangerine juice and ¼ cup of the vermouth marinade, and simmer until reduced by two-thirds.
- Add the demi-glace, and simmer for several minutes. Stir the unsalted butter into the simmering sauce until it is completely emulsified. Season to taste with salt and pepper.
- Strain the sauce through a fine sieve. Set aside 12 raspberries and 8 trimmed tangerine segments, and add the remaining berries and segments to the sauce.

TO SERVE
- Cut the breasts into thin slices, on a slight angle, across their widths. Arrange the slices on 4 appropriate serving plates. Top each serving with ¼ to ⅓ cup of sauce, and garnish with 3 raspberries, 2 tangerine segments, and fresh watercress.

Wine recommendation: light Pinot Noir

Duck Breasts and Sausages, Rhubarb Compote

Four Servings

FOR THE COMPOTE

1 cup fresh ripe
    strawberries, rinsed,
    hulled, and quartered
1 cup ¼-inch-thick, bias-
    sliced rhubarb stalks
3 tablespoons unsalted
    butter

3 tablespoons honey
juice of 1 lemon
½ teaspoon grated fresh
    ginger root

Pork caul is the thin membrane surrounding a pig's stomach. If it is unavailable, simply form the sausage mixture into 3-ounce patties, instead.

FOR THE SAUSAGES

legs and thighs of 2 ducks, boned, skinned, and cut into ¼-inch pieces
6 ounces ground pork
¼ cup chopped toasted filberts
⅛ cup "craisins" (dried cranberries)
6 fresh mint leaves
½ teaspoon salt
½ teaspoon pepper
¼ cup very cold water
8 pieces of pork caul, approximately 5 by 5 inches
vegetable oil as needed

FOR THE DUCK

4 boneless duck breasts, skin on
salt, pepper, and vegetable oil as needed

TO PREPARE THE COMPOTE

• Sauté the strawberries and rhubarb in the butter. Add the remaining ingredients, and simmer for 5 minutes. Set aside.

TO PREPARE THE SAUSAGES

• Place the duck and the pork meat in the freezer for 1 hour, then puree in a food processor along with the filberts, "craisins," mint, salt, pepper, and water until well blended.
• Preheat an oven to 375° F.
• Wrap 3-ounce portions of the sausage farce in the pork caul. Brush the sausages with oil, place in a baking pan, and roast for 10 minutes.

TO PREPARE THE DUCK

• Heat a sauté pan over a medium-high flame. Season the breasts lightly with salt and pepper, and brush lightly with oil. Sauté the breasts, skin side down, for 5 minutes. Turn them over, and continue cooking for 2 more minutes. Remove from heat, and allow to rest for 5 minutes.
• Slice the duck breasts lengthwise into thin strips. Place 2 sausages slightly off center on each of 4 serving plates, and arrange duck strips in a fan shape radiating from the sausages. Serve with a side of the compote.

Wine recommendation: Pinot Noir

VEAL AND BEEF

Veal Roulades

Four Servings

4 5-ounce slices of veal top round, pounded very thin
salt and pepper as needed
4 paper-thin slices prosciutto
4 ½-ounce slices Swiss cheese
12 large spinach leaves, blanched in boiling salted water for 30 seconds, drained, and dried

4 gherkins, sliced in half lengthwise
1 garlic clove, minced
3 tablespoons olive oil
flour as needed
½ cup chicken stock
2 tablespoons unsalted butter

- Sprinkle the veal slices lightly with salt and pepper. Place a slice of prosciutto, a slice of cheese, one-quarter of the spinach and garlic, and one split gherkin in the center of each. Roll up the veal slices, and tie them at both ends with cotton string or butcher's twine.
- Heat the olive oil in a skillet or sauté pan. Dust the roulades lightly with flour, then lightly brown them in the oil. Pour off the excess oil, add the chicken stock, cover and simmer for 5 minutes.
- Remove the roulades from the pan. Add the butter, and stir continuously until fully emulsified.
- Remove the string from the roulades, then cut each one in half at a sharp angle. Place two cut roulades on each of four serving plates, and top with the sauce.

Wine recommendation: light Beaujolais or grenache

Although professional cooks have many different ways of determining the doneness of a roast, using a meat thermometer is the least tricky. For the most accurate reading, the thermometer should be inserted into the center of a roast (or the meaty part of a chicken's thigh). Some types can be left in the meat during the entire roasting process; others cannot stand the heat. All have gauges indicating the temperatures associated with different degrees of doneness, although it is best not to follow these too slavishly.

Roast Fillet of Beef, Provence Style, with Duchess Red Bell Pepper Potatoes

Four Servings

FOR THE POTATOES

2 pounds red potatoes	2 tablespoons butter
1 medium red bell pepper	salt and white pepper to
4 large egg yolks	taste

FOR THE SAUCE

1 shallot, minced	1 cup dry white wine
3 tablespoons unsalted butter	1 tablespoon chopped fresh basil
2 garlic cloves, minced	1 tablespoon chopped fresh parsley
3 medium ripe tomatoes, peeled, cored, seeded, and cut into ¼-inch dice	salt and pepper as needed

FOR THE BEEF

1 2-pound beef tenderloin fillet, trimmed of all fat and sinew	1 garlic clove, minced
	salt, pepper, and olive oil as needed

TO PREPARE THE POTATOES

- Preheat an oven to 400° F.
- Peel the potatoes, cut into quarters, and boil until tender in lightly salted water. Drain, and set aside.
- Roast the bell pepper until the skin begins to turn black. Remove it from the oven, place it in a plastic bag, and twist the bag closed. Set aside for 10 minutes.
- Reduce the temperature setting of the oven to 350° F.
- Take the pepper from the bag, tear it open, and remove the seeds and skin from the flesh. Puree the pepper flesh with the egg yolks in a blender.
- Puree the potatoes using a potato ricer, food mill, or hand electric mixer, then thoroughly blend in the pepper-yolk mixture, butter, salt, and pepper. There should be no lumps in the puree.
- Transfer the puree to a pastry bag fitted with a large (No. 2) star tip, and pipe 8 cone-shaped forms onto a buttered baking sheet. Bake for 10 or 15 minutes, or until golden brown.

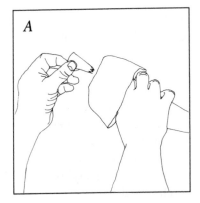

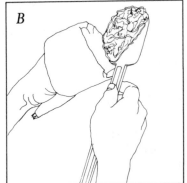

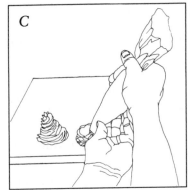

Insert a star tube into a pastry bag
(*A*). Fill the pastry bag with the
potato puree (*B*). Pipe out the
potato puree (*C*).

TO PREPARE THE SAUCE
- Sauté the shallots in 1 tablespoon of the butter for several
  minutes. Add the garlic, and sauté a few minutes longer.
  Add the tomatoes and wine, and simmer until reduced by
  half.
- Add the herbs and remaining butter, and stir continuously
  until the butter is completely incorporated. Season to taste
  with salt and pepper. Set aside.

TO PREPARE THE BEEF
- Preheat an oven to 400° F.
- Rub the fillet with the garlic, season with salt and pepper,
  then brush with olive oil.
- Roast for about 30 minutes for rare, about 40 minutes for
  medium rare. Remove, and allow to rest for 10 or 15 minutes before serving.
- Slice the fillet into ¼-inch-thick slices, and arrange on a
  serving platter or on individual serving plates. Top with the
  sauce, and garnish with the Duchess Pepper Potatoes.

Wine recommendation: rich cabernet or zinfandel

Blueberry vinegar may be difficult to find, and, since this ingredient is important to this dish, you may wish to create your own. Simply place about half a cup of rinsed and sorted blueberries in a clean wine bottle, then fill the bottle to the top with a good-quality wine vinegar or cider vinegar. Cork the bottle, and store it at room temperature in a dark area. In a few days, the vinegar will become infused with the flavor of the blueberries. Use the vinegar in this dish, in poultry and duck recipes, and in salad dressings where the flavor of blueberries will be a welcome addition. Additional vinegar can be added periodically to replace what has been used. After several refills, discard the blueberries, and start a new batch.

Infusions of this kind can be made with any kind of fruit, spice, or herb: raspberries, fresh currants, orange or lemon rind, thyme, tarragon, basil, garlic, ginger, and so on. Oil infusions can also be made in the same manner, using a good-quality olive oil and any herb or spice.

Calves' Liver
with Blueberry Vinegar and Watercress

Four Servings

8 3-ounce thin slices calves' liver
salt, pepper, and flour as needed
¼ cup olive oil
1 medium Spanish onion, sliced paper-thin

⅓ cup dry red wine
3 tablespoons blueberry vinegar
leaves of 1 bunch watercress, roughly chopped

- Season the liver slices with salt and pepper, then dust with flour.
- Heat the oil in a skillet or sauté pan, and sauté the liver slices lightly on both sides. Set aside on a plate.
- Place the onions in the pan, cover, and sauté over low heat for 7 or 8 minutes. Deglaze with the red wine and blueberry vinegar. Add the watercress leaves and the liver slices, and simmer for 2 or 3 minutes. Adjust the seasoning. Serve 2 slices per person, accompanied by the sauce.

Wine recommendation: Pinot Noir

Final Courses

COLD DESSERTS

Peach Strudel, Gingered English Cream

Four Servings

FOR THE STRUDEL
leaves from 1 bunch fresh
  mint
1 cup granulated sugar
2 cups water
4 fresh, ripe freestone
  peaches, peeled and cut
  into 12 wedges each

5 sheets phyllo dough,
  thawed
½ cup melted unsalted
  butter

FOR THE CREAM
4 large egg yolks
⅓ cup granulated sugar
1 tablespoon grated fresh
  ginger root

2 cups milk

FOR SERVING
powdered sugar

TO PREPARE THE STRUDEL
- Set aside 8 mint leaves, and roughly chop the rest.
- Bring the sugar, water, and mint to a boil in a saucepan. Add the peach wedges, and simmer until tender but still firm. Leaving the peaches in the pan, set aside until ready to serve.
- Preheat an oven to 350° F.

This dish diverges considerably from traditional strudel, sometimes referred to as the national dish of Bavaria. It is a variation of a true strudel, using the same elements but arranging them differently.

- Brush 1 sheet of phyllo lightly with melted butter. Lay a second sheet on top, and brush with butter. Repeat until 5 sheets have been buttered and stacked.
- Cut 4 4-by-3-inch rectangles from the phyllo. Place on a baking sheet, and bake for 10 minutes, or until golden brown. Remove from the oven, and set aside until ready to serve.

TO PREPARE THE CREAM
- In a small mixing bowl, whip the egg yolks with the sugar and ginger until they are thick and light lemon colored.
- Heat the milk until it just begins to simmer. Ladle it very slowly into the whipped eggs, stirring continuously. Pour this mixture into the pan, and heat over a medium flame, stirring continuously with a wooden spoon, until the mixture is slightly thickened and smooth and coats the back of the spoon. Chill for 2 hours.

TO SERVE
- For each serving, ladle about ¼ cup of the sauce onto a serving plate. Arrange 12 peach wedges on the sauce in a pinwheel shape. Top the peach wedges with a phyllo rectangle, sprinkle with powdered sugar, and garnish with fresh mint leaves.

The Carnelian Room is a restaurant on the fifty-second floor of the Bank of America Building in San Francisco. For dinner and brunch reservations, telephone (415) 433-7500.

Strawberries Carnelian

Four Servings

¾ cup port
2 tablespoons Armagnac or cognac
¼ cup Madeira
2 drops vanilla extract
¼ cup granulated sugar
juice of 1 lemon

20 large ripe strawberries, rinsed in cold water and hulled
¾ cup heavy cream, whipped
8 fresh mint leaves

- Combine the port, Armagnac, Madeira, vanilla, sugar, and lemon juice in a bowl. Add the strawberries, toss gently, and allow them to macerate ½ hour. Serve over vanilla ice cream, garnished with a dollop of whipped cream and 2 mint leaves.

Fruit Sabayon

Eight Servings

an assortment of 5 or 6
    seasonal fruits, sufficient
    for 8 servings
    (strawberries,
    blackberries, kiwis,
    peaches, nectarines, pears,
    bananas, apricots, melon,
    pineapple, oranges,
    grapefruits, etc.) cut into
    a variety of shapes and
    sizes (wedges, round
    slices, large julienne,
    small balls, etc.) and
    chilled for 1 hour

6 large egg yolks
6 tablespoons granulated
    sugar
⅔ cup marsala

- Arrange the fruit attractively in 8 champagne glasses.
- Place the remaining ingredients in a stainless steel bowl, and set this in a pan of barely simmering water. Whip vigorously with a whisk or hand electric mixer until the yolk foams up and thickens (about 5 or 7 minutes). Pour over the fresh fruit, and serve.

An alternative way of serving this dish is to ladle the sauce onto each serving plate, then place each plate under the broiler for 30 to 60 seconds, or until the sauce has turned a golden brown. Remove the plates, arrange the fruit on top of the sauce, and serve.

Sabayon is a French corruption of the Italian zabaione (the American spelling, zabaglione, is considered archaic in Italy). In France, it can be either sweet or savory—in the latter form, as an herb- and stock-flavored sauce for any variety of dishes. The Italian version is exclusively sweet, often served alone or with one or two simple cookies.

Brandied Peaches in Pastry Tulips

Four Servings

FOR THE TULIPS
⅔ cup granulated sugar
½ cup egg whites
½ cup melted unsalted
    butter

¾ cup plus 2 tablespoons
    flour

FOR THE PEACHES
½ cup brandy
1½ cups water
¼ cup granulated sugar

4 ripe medium freestone
    peaches, peeled and pitted

FOR SERVING

½ cup heavy cream
3 tablespoons Grand
  Marnier

¼ cup slivered almonds,
  toasted
8 fresh mint leaves

TO PREPARE THE TULIPS

- Preheat an oven to 400° F.
- Using a hand electric mixer, beat the sugar and egg whites in a bowl, then beat in the butter and flour just until thoroughly blended. Do not overmix.
- Place 2 tablespoons of the batter on a lightly buttered baking sheet, and spread this out into approximately a 5-inch circle. Repeat until there are 5 or 6 circles. (Only 2 or 3 circles may fit on the baking sheet; if so, repeat this procedure as needed.) Bake for 8 to 10 minutes, or until lightly browned all over and golden brown at the edges.
- Remove from the oven, and very carefully lift a circle from the sheet, using a metal spatula. Place it gently over an inverted soup or coffee cup. Repeat for each circle. The warm, soft pastry will fall over the sides of the cups and harden as it cools, when the tulips can be removed gently from their cups, inverted, and set aside.

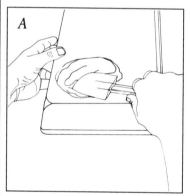

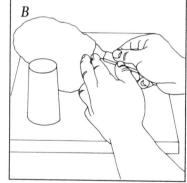

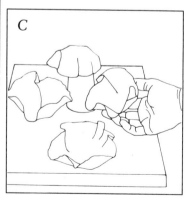

Spread a 5-inch circle of batter (A). Place the baked circle over an inverted cup (B). Gently lift off the completed tulip (C).

TO PREPARE THE PEACHES
• Bring the brandy, water, and sugar to a boil. Simmer the peaches in this syrup until they are tender but still firm. Remove from the fire, and set aside, leaving the peaches in the syrup.

TO SERVE
• Whip the cream with the Grand Marnier until it forms stiff peaks.
• Place the tulips on small plates, and place 2 peach halves in each one. Top with whipped cream, and garnish with slivered almonds and mint leaves.

Apple, Orange, and Banana Frappe

Four Servings

juice of 10 oranges
1 medium banana, peeled
1 cup apple juice
8 fresh mint leaves

8 paper-thin slices of orange, seeded
1 cup crushed ice

• Place all of the ingredients except for 4 mint leaves and the orange slices in a blender, and process at high speed until fully pureed.
• Pour into 4 large wine, or tall highball, glasses, and garnish each serving with a sprig of fresh mint, and 2 slices of orange.

Mango and White Chocolate Mousse

Six Servings

FOR THE MOUSSE
⅓ cup granulated sugar
4 large egg whites
¼ ounce (1 package) unflavored granulated gelatin
3½ ounces white chocolate, grated or minced very fine

1½ cups pureed mango
2 tablespoons dark rum
juice of ½ lemon
1½ cups heavy cream, whipped

According to the 1935 edition of Fannie Merritt Farmer's The Boston Cooking School Cookbook, *"Ices, sherbets, and frappés are generally made of fruit juices sweetened and combined with water, milk, or cream. Frappés (or sorbets) are frozen to a mush, using equal parts ice and salt." The origin of* frappe *is probably the French verb* frapper, *one sense of which means "to ice a liquid."*

FOR SERVING

¼ cup water

1 heaping tablespoon
  granulated sugar

zest of 1 lime

6 fresh mint leaves

Be sure that there are no traces of egg yolk in the egg whites and that the stainless steel bowl is completely clean and free of grease. Any fat will prevent the whites from whipping up.

TO PREPARE THE MOUSSE

- Place the sugar and egg whites in a stainless steel mixing bowl. While stirring, sprinkle in the gelatin, being careful not to let the gelatin form lumps. Place the bowl over a pan of simmering water, and whip the mixture into a foam (about 5 minutes). Remove from the simmering water.
- Stir in the bits of white chocolate until they have melted completely, then thoroughly blend in the mango puree, rum, and lemon juice. Allow to cool.
- Set aside approximately ⅓ cup of whipped cream. Fold the remaining whipped cream into the cooled mixture. When the mixture is completely homogeneous, spoon or pipe it into 6 large wine glasses. Cover, and refrigerate for 3 hours.

TO SERVE

- Bring the water and sugar to a boil. Add the lime zest, and simmer for 3 minutes. Strain, discard the syrup, and set the zest aside to cool.
- Top each glass of mousse with a tablespoon of the reserved whipped cream, a mint leaf, and a pinch of the candied lime zest.

WARM DESSERTS

Raspberry and Orange Soufflé

Six Servings

6 large juice oranges

½ cup water

6 large eggs, separated

½ cup granulated sugar

½ cup fresh raspberries

powdered sugar as needed

- Preheat an oven to 325° F.
- Cut off the top of each orange at a point where it is roughly two-and-one-half inches in diameter. Set the tops aside. Cut

a very thin slice from the bottom of each orange so that the oranges will sit firmly and not roll.

- Scoop out the pulp, then, using a rubber spatula, press it through a fine strainer. Place the juice into a small saucepan, and simmer until reduced by half. Remove from the fire, and set aside.
- Remove 1 tablespoon of orange zest from the tops, and boil in the ½ cup of water for 5 minutes. Drain the zest, and set it aside.
- Using a hand electric mixer, beat the egg yolks with the sugar in a mixing bowl until light and doubled in volume. Pour in the orange juice reduction, then add the raspberries, and continue whipping until the mixture is thoroughly blended.
- In a stainless steel bowl, whip the egg whites until they form stiff peaks.
- Thoroughly fold half of the whites into the yolks. Add the zest and remaining whites and gently fold until completely blended. Fill the orange shells with this mixture, place them on a baking sheet, and bake for 20 minutes. Sprinkle with powdered sugar.

Strawberries in Beer Batter, Sabayon Sauce

Four Servings

FOR THE BATTER
1 12-ounce bottle of beer
2 tablespoons vegetable oil
pinch salt
2 large eggs, separated

2½ cups flour
2 tablespoons granulated sugar

FOR THE SAUCE
5 large egg yolks
⅔ cup granulated sugar
1 cup dry white wine
1 tablespoon kirsch

¼ teaspoon vanilla
½ teaspoon lemon zest
1 teaspoon orange zest

FOR THE STRAWBERRIES
16 extra-large or 20 medium long-stem strawberries, rinsed in cold water

flour as needed
powdered sugar as needed

Soufflé is the past participle of the French verb soufffler, meaning "to whisper, to blow, to breathe"— an indication of the dish's well-known fragility. Making a successful soufflé seems to be the quintessential culinary challenge, and a failed soufflé may signal a failed chef. Part of the problem is that this eighteenth-century relative of genoise, a light sponge cake, must be baked at a temperature high enough to set the proteins in the egg but low enough to heat the interior without burning the exterior. At 325° F, you should have good results.

Of course, a soufflé inevitably will begin to fall once it is removed from the oven, and opening the oven door prematurely, to see if a soufflé is done, can be dangerous. For this dish, we suggest that you check ever so cautiously only at the fifteen-minute mark, the minimum amount of time in which these soufflés will cook. If they have risen and sufficiently browned at that point, be sure to deliver them to the dining table as soon as possible and with as little brusque movement as you can manage. And it always helps to have a spectacular back-up dessert on hand, just in case.

If there is any soufflé mixture remaining after the shells have been filled, butter a couple of ceramic ramekins or soufflé dishes, fill them with the remaining soufflé, and bake them along with the orange shells.

TO PREPARE THE BATTER
- Pour the beer into a mixing bowl. Add the oil, salt, and egg yolks. Beat well.
- Beat in the flour slowly until the mixture is smooth.
- In a separate bowl, beat the egg whites, adding the sugar slowly, until they form stiff peaks.
- Fold the egg whites into the beer mixture until they are incorporated fully. Set the batter aside to rest for 30 minutes.

TO PREPARE THE SAUCE
- Place all of the sauce ingredients in a stainless steel mixing bowl over a pan of simmering water. Whip the sauce mixture continuously until it is thickened (8 to 10 minutes). Set aside, keeping it warm.

TO PREPARE THE STRAWBERRIES
- Preheat an oven to 200° F.
- Heat 2 inches of vegetable oil to 360° F in a heavy-gauge pot. (Use a candy thermometer to determine the temperature.)
- Dust the strawberries lightly with flour, then dip them in the batter, allowing the excess to drip off.
- Fry the strawberries in the hot oil until they are golden brown. Drain on absorbent paper, placing them in the oven to keep warm until all the berries are fried.
- For each serving, place ¼ cup of sabayon sauce on a small serving plate. Top with 4 or 5 strawberries, and sprinkle with powdered sugar.

AUTUMN

First Courses

COLD APPETIZERS

Tuna Carpaccio with Toast Points

Four Servings

5 ounces fresh boneless, skinless tuna
3 tablespoons vinegar, cider or white wine
1 tablespoon dry sherry
2 tablespoons olive oil

1 tablespoon chopped fresh tarragon leaves
4 slices fresh white bread
1 head Bibb lettuce
¼ cup ⅛-inch-diced red bell pepper

- Place the tuna in the freezer for 1 hour.
- Slice the tuna across the grain into paper-thin slices.
- In a small bowl, mix the vinegar, sherry, oil, and tarragon. Add the tuna slices, cover, and refrigerate for 3 hours.
- Trim the crusts from the sliced bread. Cut each slice diagonally, and toast.
- Remove the outermost dark green leaves from the lettuce, and reserve for another salad. Cut the core from the lettuce heart.
- Place a leaf of lettuce heart on each toast triangle. Top with a slice of tuna, then a sprinkle of red pepper.

Wine recommendation: crisp sauvignon blanc

Wild Mushroom Terrine, Red Pepper Aioli

About Fifteen Servings

FOR THE AIOLI
2 large egg yolks
1 large red bell pepper,
  roasted and peeled
4 large garlic cloves, minced

salt and pepper as needed
1 cup olive oil
juice of 1 lemon

FOR THE TERRINE
1½ pounds fresh lobster
  mushrooms
1 small shallot, minced
1 tablespoon unsalted butter
1 teaspoon salt
½ teaspoon white pepper
½ cup dry white wine
1 pound boneless, skinless
  chicken breast meat, cut
  into ¼-inch pieces

1 small egg
1½ cups heavy cream
1½ teaspoons fresh thyme
  leaves
1 ear of corn, blanched in
  boiling salted water,
  kernels removed

FOR SERVING
15 sprigs fresh thyme
60 French bread slices,
  toasted

TO PREPARE THE AIOLI
- Puree the egg yolks, bell pepper, and garlic thoroughly in a food processor. Season lightly with salt and pepper.
- Using the pulse switch on the food processor, alternately add the olive oil and the lemon juice to this mixture. Pour the oil slowly, making sure that each addition is fully incorporated before adding more. Season to taste with salt and pepper.

TO PREPARE THE TERRINE
- Blanch the mushrooms in lightly salted boiling water for 5 minutes. Drain, and pat them dry. Set aside 8 whole mushrooms, and finely chop the rest in a food processor.
- Sauté the chopped mushrooms and the shallot in the butter for 5 minutes over high heat. Add the salt, pepper, and white wine. Simmer, reducing the mixture until it is almost completely dry.

Aioli is a Mediterranean variation on mayonnaise. The important thing to remember when making mayonnaise is to pour the oil very slowly into the egg yolks, continuously beating the mixture in order to incorporate the oil. If the oil is added too fast, the yolks cannot absorb it, and the result is a broken sauce, remedied only by starting from the beginning with new egg yolks.

See Roast Potatoes and Bell Peppers (Spring, First Courses, page 17) for instructions on how to roast the pepper.

- Place the chicken meat in the freezer for approximately 1 hour, or until it is partially frozen. Then place it in a food processor with the egg, and puree. Next, continuing to puree, add the cream in a slow, steady stream. Fold in the sautéed mushrooms, thyme, and corn kernels. Cover, and place in the refrigerator until ready to bake.
- Preheat an oven to 300° F. Butter the interior of a 1½-quart pâté mold.
- Pack half of the chicken farce into the mold, pressing down firmly. Arrange the reserved mushrooms on top of this, then add the remaining farce, again pressing down firmly. Cover with a sheet of buttered parchment paper cut to the size of the top surface.
- Place the mold in a deep roasting pan, and then place this in the oven. Pour enough very hot water into the pan to reach roughly halfway up the mold, and bake for 50 minutes. Remove, allow to cool to room temperature, then refrigerate overnight.

TO SERVE
- When ready to serve, set the mold in a pan of very hot water for a moment. Remove, dry off the outside, then invert the mold over a plate, and remove the terrine.
- Slice the terrine. For each serving, place 3 slices on a serving plate, spoon on a dollop of the aioli, and garnish with a sprig of fresh thyme and 4 slices of toasted baguette.

Wine recommendation: cabernet sauvignon

HOT APPETIZERS

Mussel Barquettes, Saffron Sauce

Four or Five Servings

FOR THE PASTRY
2 cups flour
¼ teaspoon salt
12 tablespoons butter (1½ sticks), cut into ½-inch cubes

2 tablespoons vegetable shortening or margarine
2 tablespoons ice water

FOR THE FILLING

1 tablespoon minced
  shallots
1 cup dry white wine
1 sprig fresh thyme
20 large mussels, debearded
  and well rinsed

pinch saffron
1 cup minced leeks, white
  part only
1 cup heavy cream
¼ cup chopped fresh chives

TO PREPARE THE PASTRY

- Combine the flour and salt in a mixing bowl. Add the butter cubes and shortening, and rub together between the fingers, until the mixture resembles coarse crumbs. Add the water, and form the mixture into a rough ball (use additional ice water, if necessary). Cover and refrigerate for 1 hour.
- Preheat an oven to 425° F.
- On a floured board, roll out the dough to a thickness of ¹⁄₁₆ inch.
- Cut 20 small portions of dough, and press each piece into a barquette mold. Trim the dough so that the edges are even with the tops of the molds, then press it gently until the trimmed edges rise a small distance above the tops. (This helps to compensate for shrinkage during baking.)

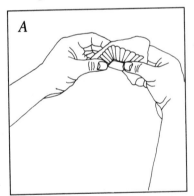

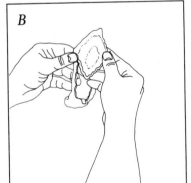

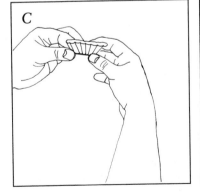

Press the dough into the barquette mold (*A*). Trim off the excess dough (*B*). Press the dough gently, so the trimmed edges rise slightly above the edge of the mold (*C*).

Dishes made from the enlarged livers of fattened geese and duck have been enjoyed as far back as ancient Roman times. The goose was considered a sacred animal by the Romans, a dubious distinction as far as the geese were concerned, given the various ways in which their livers were grossly fattened to produce this gastronomic delicacy. Until recently, the finest foie gras—literally "fat liver"—came from the Alsatian and southwestern regions of France. Austria, Czechoslovakia, Luxembourg, and, more recently, Israel also produce an excellent foie gras.

In the early 1980s, Rubin Josephs and his son Howard began to raise a crossbred Muscovy and Pekin duck on their farm in Mongaup Valley, New York. Unlike the traditional French practice of force-feeding the individually caged birds—something animal rights activists and animal lovers in general abhor —the Josephs method allows the ducks to range free within open-air pens. Before the Josephs ventured into domestic foie gras production, only imported foie gras was available in the United States, either cooked or canned. Now, some of the finest chefs and restaurateurs in the United States are raving about this fresh, raw, vacuum-packed liver, reportedly as rich, smooth, and flavorful as any produced overseas. The Josephs also sell whole ducks, breasts, and legs, fresh or smoked, as well as giblets and rendered fat.

- Bake for 10 minutes. Remove, and set aside.

TO PREPARE THE FILLING
- Bring the shallots, wine, and thyme to a boil. Add the mussels, cover, and simmer until all the mussel shells are open. Remove the mussels from the pan.
- Add the saffron and the leeks to the wine mixture, and simmer until almost dry. Add the cream, and reduce by half.
- Remove the mussels from their shells, and add them to the sauce. Stir, and remove from the fire. Place a teaspoon or so of the sauce into each barquette shell, making sure to include a mussel. Heat in a 350° F oven for about 5 minutes. Sprinkle with chopped chives, and serve.

Wine recommendation: crisp chardonnay

New York State Foie Gras and Wild Mushrooms, Cider Sauce

Four Servings

FOR THE SAUCE

1 large shallot, minced
2 tablespoons unsalted butter
½ cup apple cider
2 tablespoons white raisins

¼ cup dry white wine
1 tablespoon curry powder
1½ cups heavy cream
salt and pepper as needed

FOR THE FOIE GRAS AND MUSHROOMS

32 fresh spinach leaves, stemmed and well washed
3 tablespoons unsalted butter
20 fresh medium shiitake mushrooms
20 fresh medium oyster mushrooms

20 fresh medium chanterelle mushrooms
8 ounces fresh foie gras, cut into 4 slices
flour as needed

TO PREPARE THE SAUCE
- Sauté the shallot in the butter for 5 minutes. Add the cider, raisins, wine, and curry powder. Simmer until reduced by two-thirds. Add the heavy cream, and reduce by one-third.

Season to taste with salt and pepper. Set aside, keeping warm.

TO PREPARE THE FOIE GRAS AND MUSHROOMS

- Sauté the spinach in 1 tablespoon of the butter for 2 or 3 minutes. Divide among 4 serving plates.
- Pour the excess butter from the pan, add a second tablespoon of butter, and sauté the mushrooms for 3 minutes. Remove from the pan, and divide equally among the 4 serving plates with the spinach.
- Dust the foie gras lightly with the flour. Pour the mushroom juices from the pan, add the last tablespoon of butter, and sauté the foie gras for a minute or two on each side.
- Place a slice of foie gras in the center of each of the 4 serving plates. Drizzle ¼ cup or so of the sauce on each, and serve.

Wine recommendation: Pinot Noir or merlot

Howard Josephs recommends that, when working with foie gras, you allow it to sit at room temperature for a half hour or so before cooking it, carefully trim it of all skin, sinew, veins and slice it (if wanted), using a knife dipped in hot water, and, because of its high fat content, cook it quickly over high heat, using little or no fat.

California Artichokes with Havarti and Cauliflower Puree

Six Servings

FOR THE PUREE

1 small head cauliflower, cut into 2-inch chunks	1 teaspoon salt
1 medium baking potato, peeled and cut in half	1 teaspoon pepper
	1 cup heavy cream
	2 tablespoons butter

FOR THE ARTICHOKES

6 medium artichokes, stems removed, cut flush with the base, and the top ¼ inch of each leaf trimmed with a scissors	1 teaspoon salt
	1 teaspoon pepper
	juice of ½ lemon
	1 cup small-diced Havarti cheese

TO PREPARE THE PUREE

- Place the potato in boiling salted water, and boil for 5 minutes. Add the cauliflower, and cook until both the potato and the cauliflower are tender. Drain completely dry.
- Puree the cauliflower, potato, salt, pepper, cream, and butter in a blender. Remove to a small bowl, and set aside.

TO PREPARE THE ARTICHOKES
- Place the artichokes in boiling water along with the salt, pepper, and lemon juice. Cook for 17 minutes, or until the artichoke bottoms are tender when pierced with a toothpick. Drain and cool.
- Preheat an oven to 350° F.
- Pull the inside center leaves from the artichoke. Using a spoon, scoop out the choke. Discard the leaves and the choke.
- Stuff the artichokes with the cauliflower puree, then top with the diced cheese. Place in a buttered baking pan, and bake for 8 to 10 minutes. Serve with a simple tossed green salad.

Grilled Shiitake Mushrooms, Miso Sauce

Four Servings

Miso is a fermented and aged soy bean paste unique to Japanese cuisine. It has a very high protein content and is often used as a substitute for meat and meat juice reductions.

FOR THE MUSHROOMS

¼ cup soy sauce, mixed with ¼ cup water
2 tablespoons honey
1 tablespoon rice wine vinegar

12 medium fresh shiitake mushrooms

FOR THE SAUCE

1 shallot, minced
6 tablespoons dry white wine
2 cups heavy cream

2 tablespoons light miso paste
1 teaspoon soy sauce
¼ teaspoon white pepper

FOR SERVING

2 tablespoons chopped fresh chives

TO PREPARE THE MUSHROOMS
- Combine the soy sauce–water mixture, honey, and vinegar. Add the mushroom caps, reserving the stems, and marinate 1 hour.

TO PREPARE THE SAUCE
- Simmer the stems, shallots, and white wine in a small saucepan until almost dry. Add the cream, miso, soy sauce, and pepper. Simmer until reduced by half. Strain and set aside.

TO SERVE
- Prepare an outdoor grill.
- Grill the shiitakes, top side down, for 2 or 3 minutes. Flip, and grill the other side. Ladle a small portion of the sauce onto appropriate serving plates. Top with the grilled mushroom caps, and sprinkle with chopped chives.

Wine recommendation: rich merlot

Asparagus and Forest Mushrooms in Phyllo, Roasted Garlic Sauce

Four Servings

You can thaw a package of phyllo sheets, take what you need, and refreeze the rest, but work quickly so that the sheets do not dry out.

FOR THE SAUCE

1 head garlic
¾ cup white wine
1 shallot, minced

1½ cups heavy cream
salt and pepper as needed

FOR THE MUSHROOMS

14 ounces assorted wild mushrooms (chanterelles, hedgehogs, boletus, black trumpets, morels, or commercially grown shiitakes, oyster mushrooms, etc.), cleaned

8 tablespoons (1 stick) butter
2 shallots, minced
salt and pepper as needed
¼ cup cognac

FOR THE PHYLLO

5 sheets phyllo dough, thawed
8 tablespoons (1 stick) butter, melted

½ bunch fresh chives, chopped

TO PREPARE THE SAUCE
- Preheat an oven to 325° F.
- Place the garlic head in a small roasting pan, and add enough water almost to cover it. Roast for 1 hour, remove, and allow to cool.
- Simmer the wine and shallot in a saucepan, reducing until almost completely dry. Squeeze the individual garlic cloves into the pan. Add the cream, and simmer until reduced by half. Puree the sauce in a blender or food processor, strain,

and season to taste with salt and pepper. Set aside, keeping the sauce warm.

TO PREPARE THE MUSHROOMS
- Sauté the mushroom pieces in the butter for 5 minutes. Add the shallots, salt, and pepper, and cook for another 3 minutes. Add the cognac, and simmer until almost completely dry. Set aside.

TO PREPARE THE PHYLLO
- Preheat an oven to 350° F.
- Brush 1 sheet of phyllo dough lightly with melted butter. Place another sheet of phyllo on top, and brush this with butter. Repeat with remaining sheets.
- Cut the stack of phyllo lengthwise into 2½- to 3-inch-wide strips. Near the end of one strip, place a heaping tablespoon of the mushroom mixture. Fold one corner over triangularly, flush with the opposite side. Fold this triangle over the filling. Continue folding this triangle to the end of the strip (see diagram). Repeat this process with the remaining strips.
- Place the filled triangles on a lightly buttered baking sheet,

Cut the phyllo dough sheets lengthwise into 4 strips (A). Fold a corner of each strip over the filling (B). Fold the first triangle up along the strip (C). Brush the triangle with melted butter (D).

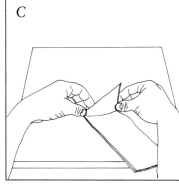

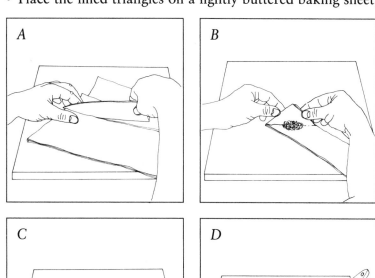

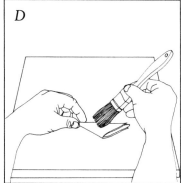

and bake until golden brown. Serve with the warm sauce, topped with chopped chives.

Wine recommendation: crisp chardonnay

Tagliarini with White Truffles

Four Servings

FOR THE PASTA
1 pound semolina flour
4 large eggs
pinch salt

1 tablespoon olive oil
all-purpose flour as needed

FOR SERVING
1 teaspoon salt
1 tablespoon olive oil
1 cup heavy cream
6 tablespoons (¾ stick) unsalted butter

salt and pepper as needed
⅓ cup grated Parmesan cheese
2 whole white truffles, sliced paper-thin

TO PREPARE THE PASTA
- Place the flour in a pile in the center of a wooden board. Make a small well in the center of the flour, and add the eggs, salt, and olive oil. Carefully blend these ingredients into the flour, and knead vigorously, until the dough is smooth and elastic. (Use additional flour during kneading, if necessary, to prevent the dough from sticking to the board.) Wrap, and allow to rest in the refrigerator for 1 hour.
- Roll out portions of the dough very thin, using a manually operated pasta machine. With the attachment for producing ⅛-inch-wide strips, cut the dough into "tagliarini." Dust these with flour to prevent them from sticking together.

TO SERVE
- Add the salt and olive oil to a gallon of water, and bring to rolling boil, bring the water back to a boil, and cook the pasta for 1 minute. Drain.
- Bring the cream to a boil in a large pan. Remove from the fire, add the pasta, butter, salt, pepper, and Parmesan cheese, and toss. Place on 4 individual serving plates. Top with the truffle slices and additional freshly ground black pepper.

Wine recommendation: high-acid Pinot Noir

If you decide to substitute a dried variety of pasta, extend the cooking time to roughly 8 minutes (until it is al dente—tender but still firm).

Always make sure that the water in which pasta is to be cooked is boiling vigorously before the pasta is added. If it is not, the pasta will have a mealy consistency.

Truffles are mycorrhizal, meaning that they have a nutritionally symbiotic relationship with a plant, in this case, conifer (evergreen) trees; thus, they are frequently found near the roots of such trees or shrubs. Tuber gibbosum, or the white truffle, is found from California to British Columbia, though it is especially common in Oregon. Often found at the base of Douglas fir trees, it measures anywhere from a half inch to two inches. Irregularly knobby, it is whitish when young, turning light beige to tan or brown as it matures. Its interior is solid, marbled, and crisp, with a strong musty and garlicky aroma when fully mature. TRUFFLE HUNTERS, BEWARE: Certain varieties of tubers and wild mushrooms can be lethally poisonous. Hunt them *ONLY* with an experienced mycologist.

SOUPS

Chilled Granny Smith Apple and Ginger Soup

Four Servings

1 cup whole fresh
  raspberries
¼ cup water
2 tablespoons granulated
  sugar
2 tablespoons Grand
  Marnier
5 Granny Smith apples, 4½
  quartered and cored,
  remaining ½ peeled,
  cored, cut into fine
  julienne, then tossed in a
  bowl with ½ cup water
  and the juice of ½ lemon

3 cups apple juice
2 tablespoons grated fresh
  ginger root
juice of 10 to 12 limes
½ cup whole fresh
  raspberries

- Bring the first 4 ingredients to a boil, and simmer for 15 minutes. Puree in a blender or food processor, then strain through a fine sieve. Cool, cover, and refrigerate.
- Place the quartered apples, apple juice, and ginger in a saucepan, bring to a boil, and simmer for 10 minutes. Puree in a blender or food processor, then strain through a fine sieve. Cool, cover, and refrigerate.
- When the apple mixture is chilled, stir in the lime juice, and pour into chilled soup plates. Make a design with raspberry puree on the surface of the apple soup, then garnish with fresh raspberries and the julienned apple.

Cold Cranberry Soup

Four to Six Servings

1 pound fresh (or fresh-
   frozen) whole cranberries
1 quart cranberry juice
1 pint dry red wine
½ cup granulated sugar
zest and juice of 1 lemon
zest and juice of 1 orange
2 2- to 3-inch cinnamon
   sticks

½ pint fresh-squeezed
   orange juice
¼ cup cornstarch, dissolved
   in ¼ cup cold water
4 tablespoons sour cream
½ ripe pear, peeled, cored,
   cut into fine julienne

- Place all but the last 3 ingredients in a small saucepan. Bring to a boil, and simmer for 15 minutes. Puree in a blender or food processor.
- Strain the puree back into the saucepan, and bring it to a simmer. Add the cornstarch dissolved in cold water, and simmer for another minute. Remove from the fire, and allow to cool, then cover, and refrigerate until fully chilled.
- Serve the soup in chilled soup plates, garnished with the sour cream and the julienned pear.

Escarole, Barley, and Smoked Turkey Soup

Six to Eight Servings

6 ounces barley
2 tablespoons butter
2 garlic cloves, minced
1 small Spanish onion,
   peeled and cut into ¼-
   inch dice
2 small carrots, peeled and
   cut into ¼-inch dice
2 stalks celery, cut into ¼-
   inch dice
1 cup medium-diced
   smoked turkey meat

6 cups chicken stock
1 sprig fresh thyme
1 teaspoon chopped fresh
   basil
1 bay leaf
¼ head escarole, well
   washed and cut into 1-
   inch pieces
salt and pepper as needed

- Bring 2 quarts of salted water to the boil. Add the barley, and cook until tender. Drain, and set aside.
- Melt the butter in a 1-gallon pot, and sauté the garlic and

onion for about 5 minutes. Add the carrots, celery, turkey, stock, and herbs. Simmer until the vegetables are tender. Add the escarole and barley, and simmer 5 more minutes. Season to taste with salt and pepper.

Sweet Potato and Leek Soup

Four Servings

3 medium leeks, trimmed of dark green tops and root, cut into ¼-inch dice, and well rinsed
3 tablespoons butter
3 medium sweet potatoes, peeled and cut into ¼-inch dice

3 cups chicken stock
1 cup heavy cream
salt and pepper to taste
½ cup finely julienned Granny Smith apple

- Sauté the leeks in the butter, covered, until they are transparent—about 8 minutes.
- Add the sweet potatoes and stock, bring to a boil, and simmer until potatoes are tender.
- Puree half of the soup mixture in a blender or food processor, and return it to the soup pot.
- Bring the soup back to a simmer, add the cream, and season to taste with salt and pepper.
- Serve in heated soup plates, topped with julienned apple.

Ginger Pumpkin Soup with Filberts

Four Servings

4 very small pumpkins
vegetable oil as needed
1 whole medium pumpkin
1 small Spanish onion, peeled and finely chopped
½ carrot, peeled and finely chopped
1 stalk celery, finely chopped

2 tablespoons butter
1 cup filberts, finely ground
½ teaspoon grated fresh ginger root
2 cups chicken stock
salt and pepper to taste
1 cup heavy cream

- Preheat an oven to 350° F.

- Cut off the tops of the small pumpkins. Scoop out the seeds and webbing from inside each one, replace the tops, and rub the outsides with oil.
- Cut the medium pumpkin in half. Scoop out and discard the seeds and webbing. Place a few tablespoons of water into each half.
- Place the pumpkin halves and the small pumpkins in a baking dish. Bake until the skin on the small pumpkins begins to turn brown and the flesh in the halves is tender. Remove from the oven. Set the small pumpkins aside, and pour off the water in the two halves, scoop out the pulp, and set aside.
- Sauté the onion, carrot, and celery in the butter for about 5 minutes. Add the pumpkin meat, filberts, ginger, and chicken stock. Simmer for 15 minutes, then season to taste with salt and pepper.
- Puree the soup in a blender or food processor, and return it to the pan. Add the cream, bring to a simmer, and adjust the seasoning. Serve the soup in the small scooped-out pumpkins.

SALADS

Autumn Greens with Pine Nuts and Mustard Vinaigrette

Four Servings

¼ cup pine nuts
a variety of fresh seasonal lettuces sufficient for 4 salads (dandelion greens, Bibb, radicchio, red leaf, endive, oriental savoy, arugula, etc.)
½ cup stemmed fresh seasonal herbs (chervil, sage, parsley, tarragon, etc.)

2 tablespoons Dijon mustard
3 tablespoons red wine vinegar
¾ cup walnut and/or olive oil
pinch salt
pinch pepper

Lettuce and fresh herbs should be rinsed thoroughly in plenty of cold water in order to remove all traces of sand, soil, and impurities. They should all be dried completely, since wet greens can water down an accompanying sauce or vinaigrette. Use a lettuce spinner for this chore, then wrap the rinsed and dried greens in a clean pillowcase or dish cloth, and place them in the refrigerator to crisp.

- Preheat an oven to 350° F.

Delicate greens such as Boston, Limestone, arugula, green leaf, and red leaf should be torn into bite-size pieces; coarser lettuces such as romaine, chicory, endive, and escarole can be cut with a knife into uniform pieces.

- Toast the pine nuts in the oven until they are golden brown. Remove, and set aside.
- Gently tear the lettuces into bite-size pieces. Rinse in cold water, spin or pat dry, and refrigerate until ready to serve.
- Rinse the herbs in cold water, spin or pat dry, then chop finely, and store in a small jar in the refrigerator until ready to serve.
- Combine the remaining ingredients in a mixing bowl, and blend thoroughly.
- Toss the greens in the vinaigrette, and arrange on individual, chilled salad plates. Top with the toasted pine nuts and the chopped herbs.

Sweet-and-Pungent Cabbage Salad

Four to Six Servings

1 small head white cabbage, sliced very thin
2 Granny Smith apples, quartered, cored, and sliced very thin
1 teaspoon grated fresh ginger root
¼ cup ½-inch-diced slab bacon

1 medium Spanish onion, cut lengthwise into thin julienne strips
4 tablespoons brown sugar
½ cup malt or cider vinegar
1 teaspoon dry mustard, dissolved in 1 tablespoon malt or cider vinegar
salt and pepper as needed

- Toss the cabbage, apples, and ginger in a salad bowl.
- Render the bacon in a sauté pan over a medium flame. Add the onion, and sauté for 5 minutes. Add the sugar and vinegar, and cook another 3 minutes.
- Blend in the dissolved mustard and remove from the fire.
- Pour the hot dressing over the cabbage and apples. Season with salt and pepper, and serve.

Watercress and Apple Salad, Raspberry Vinaigrette

Four Servings

The raspberry vinaigrette recipe yields a little more than a cup of dressing, which may be more then you will need for the salad. You can use as much or as little as you prefer and store any leftover vinaigrette in a covered jar in the refrigerator for future use.

FOR THE VINAIGRETTE
1 small shallot, minced
¾ cup vegetable oil
¼ cup raspberry vinegar
pinch salt
pinch white pepper

FOR THE SALAD
2 bunches fresh watercress, stems removed and leaves well washed
2 large heads Belgian endive, bottoms trimmed and leaves separated and washed
1 Granny Smith apple, peeled, cored, cut into 24 wedges, then held in a bath of 1 cup cold water mixed with the juice of 1 lemon
16 fresh raspberries

TO PREPARE THE VINAIGRETTE
• Blend all the vinaigrette ingredients together in a small bowl. Cover, and refrigerate until ready to serve.

TO PREPARE THE SALAD
• Arrange the watercress in the center of 4 chilled salad plates. Arrange the endive leaves radially around the watercress. Drain and dry the apple wedges. Sprinkle the apple wedges and raspberries over the top of the greens. Stir up the vinaigrette, and spoon it over the salad.

Purple Artichoke and Arugula Salad

Four Servings

Arugula and some herb varieties are not always available in every autumn market. When this is the case, substitute other varieties of locally grown lettuce or salad herbs.

FOR THE DRESSING
6 tablespoons balsamic vinegar
¾ cup olive oil
1 shallot, minced
pinch salt
pinch pepper

Balsamic vinegar is an aged Italian white wine vinegar that gains its dark brown color during its prolonged contact with the wooden barrels in which it is aged. Some balsamic vinegars are aged for as long as one hundred years.

FOR THE SALAD

4 small purple artichokes, with stems intact

¾ cup dry white wine

¼ cup peeled and diced ripe tomato

2 tablespoons olive oil

juice of 1 lemon

1 garlic clove, minced

1 tablespoon fresh thyme leaves

2 bunches fresh arugula, rinsed, dried, and torn into bite-size pieces

2 tablespoons chopped fresh mixed herbs (parsley, basil, thyme, and tarragon)

TO PREPARE THE DRESSING
- Puree all the ingredients in a blender.

TO PREPARE THE SALAD
- Split the artichokes in half lengthwise, and place them in a stainless steel saucepan along with the wine, tomato, oil, lemon juice, garlic, and thyme. Bring to a boil, cover, and simmer for 15 to 20 minutes, or until the artichokes are tender. Allow the artichokes to cool to room temperature in the poaching liquid.
- Toss the arugula in the vinaigrette. Arrange on individual, chilled serving plates. Place two artichoke halves on top of the greens on each plate, and pour a tablespoon of the poaching liquid on each half. Sprinkle with the fresh herbs and serve.

Main Courses

FISH

Salmon with Grainy Mustard, Avocado Salsa

Four Servings

If you prefer less peppery dishes, you may wish to reduce the quantity of cracked black peppercorns.

FOR THE SALSA

1 small cucumber, peeled, seeded, and cut into ⅛-inch dice

1 ripe medium tomato, peeled, seeded, and cut into ⅛-inch dice

1 small Bermuda onion, cut into ⅛-inch dice

1 small yellow or red bell pepper, cut into ⅛-inch dice

½ cup fresh lime juice

3 tablespoons chopped fresh cilantro

1 tablespoon olive oil

salt to taste

1 ripe avocado

FOR THE SALMON

4 tablespoons grainy mustard

4 6-ounce salmon fillets, skinned

2 teaspoons cracked black peppercorns

¼ cup olive oil

TO PREPARE THE SALSA

- Combine all the ingredients except the avocado in a small bowl. Cover, and allow to marinate at room temperature for 2 hours.
- Peel the avocado, cut it into ¼-inch dice, and toss it thoroughly with the marinating vegetables. Set the salsa aside.

TO PREPARE THE SALMON
- Spread a thin coat of mustard on both sides of the salmon fillets. Sprinkle both sides with the cracked black pepper.
- Heat a sauté pan over a medium-high flame. Add the oil. When hot, add the fillets, flesh side down, and sauté until golden brown. Turn over, and cook another 2 minutes. Remove to serving plates. Serve with the salsa.

Wine recommendation: rich sauvignon blanc

Grilled Swordfish, Ginger Sauce and Cranberry Compote

Four Servings

FOR THE COMPOTE

1 cup whole fresh (or fresh-frozen) cranberries	¼ cup zinfandel or other dry red wine
2 tablespoons granulated sugar	zest of ½ orange 2 whole cloves

FOR THE SAUCE

3 tablespoons grated fresh ginger root	8 tablespoons (1 stick) unsalted butter, cut into ½-inch cubes
¼ cup dry white wine	
1 shallot, minced	salt and pepper as needed
½ cup heavy cream	

FOR THE FISH

4 7- to 8-ounce swordfish steaks	salt, pepper, and vegetable oil as needed

TO PREPARE THE COMPOTE
- Combine the cranberries, sugar, red wine, zest, and cloves in a saucepan. Bring to a boil, and simmer for 10 minutes. Set aside.

TO PREPARE THE SAUCE
- Combine the ginger, wine, and shallot in a saucepan. Bring to a simmer, and reduce until almost completely dry. Add the cream, simmer, and reduce by half.
- Add the butter, a couple of cubes at a time, stirring continuously until it is fully incorporated. Remove from the fire, and season to taste with salt and pepper. Set aside.

In the early 1900s, cranberries were still a fresh-produce business, and what didn't sell, rotted. Marcus L. Urann, a New England lawyer and something of an eccentric, decided to do something about this. He came up with a recipe for a processed cranberry sauce, and, in 1912, he founded the Ocean Spray Preserving Company and began production. After World War I, other companies entered the processed cranberry business, most notably the A. D. Makepeace Company of Wareham, Massachusetts, and the Cranberry Products Company of New Egypt, New Jersey. In 1930, these three companies merged to form the cranberry growers' cooperative now known as Ocean Spray Cranberries, Inc. In 1977, Ocean Spray established the Cranberry World Museum in the town of Plymouth, Massachusetts. Only a ten-minute walk from Plymouth Rock, it is well worth a visit. For further information, contact Cranberry World Museum, 225 Water Street, Plymouth, MA 02360, telephone (508) 747-2350.

TO PREPARE THE FISH
- Prepare an outdoor grill.
- Season the swordfish steaks lightly with salt and pepper, then coat them lightly with vegetable oil.
- Grill the steaks 5 to 7 minutes on each side, until they are fully cooked.
- Remove the steaks to an appropriate serving plate. Ladle approximately ¼ cup of warm sauce over each steak. Serve with a side of the compote.

Wine recommendation: light Pinot Noir or Beaujolais

SHELLFISH

Prawns with Tangerine and Riesling

Four Servings

2 shallots, minced	juice of 1 tangerine
2 tablespoons butter	1 cup heavy cream
2 tablespoons olive oil	salt and pepper as needed
16 large prawns, shelled and deveined, tails removed	12 sprigs fresh watercress
	12 tangerine segments, trimmed and seeded
1 cup Riesling	

- Sauté the shallots in the butter and oil for 3 minutes. Add the prawns, and sauté for another minute or two. Remove the prawns, and set them aside.
- Add the wine and tangerine juice to the pan, and simmer until almost dry. Add the cream, and reduce by half. Return the prawns and their juices to the pan, bring to a simmer, and season to taste with salt and pepper.
- Arrange the prawns radially on individual serving plates, with the tail ends at the center of the plates. Top with the sauce, and garnish with watercress and tangerine segments.

Wine recommendation: dry Riesling

Shrimp belong to the order Decapoda, which includes any crustacean with five pairs of locomotor appendages (legs), each joined at the thorax (the middle section of their bodies). Crabs, lobsters, prawns, shrimp, squid, and cuttlefish are all decapods.

The term prawn generally is used to refer to very large shrimp and to species of freshwater shrimp. Dublin Bay prawns, however, are actually small, spiny lobsters, as are the Italian scampi—making the name of the dish "shrimp scampi," already redundant, a misnomer as well. The waters of the North Pacific off North America, however, do boast a prawn that reaches a length of as much as 9 inches.

In the United States, it seems that Easterners always call a shrimp a shrimp, while prawn is used in the West. Whatever they are called, several hundred species of shrimp and/or prawns are found in shallow water over muddy bottoms and in deep northern ocean waters all over the planet. They are highly perishable, decaying quickly after harvesting. Thus, they only became highly prized gastronomically, and their harvesting a major industry, after the advent of offshore trawlers in about 1917.

The world's richest shrimp waters are in the Gulf of Mexico, so it is no wonder that the United States is the largest consumer of shrimp—we eat about 500 million pounds of them a year, with New York City alone accounting for nearly 80 million pounds.

Truffles are a curious food, fabled for centuries for their mystical and aphrodisiac qualities. Brillat-Savarin called them "the diamonds of cookery"; in Italian, they are called perle della cucina— *"pearls of the kitchen"; the Roman satirist Juvenal told the Libyans in the first century, "Keep your wheat, and send us your truffles!"*

The word truffle *is derived from the Spanish* trufa *or the Italian* truffere, *both meaning "deceit," probably in reference to the fact that this variety of wild mushroom grows just underneath the surface of the ground and is thus difficult to locate. Since humans do not possess a keen olfactory sense, we elicit help. In Sardinia, goats are employed to track down truffles; bear cubs have been used in Russia; and pigs and specially trained dogs do the job in Europe. Pigs are the real experts, for the most basic of reasons: the aroma of truffles is similar to one particular pig sex hormone and sends them into a lustful frenzy when their sharp noses detect the little tuber. Both pigs and dogs can detect truffles from as far away as 50 yards.*

Scallops with Shiitakes and Oregon Truffles

Four Servings

3 shallots, minced
2 garlic cloves, minced
3 tablespoons olive oil
2 cups shiitake mushrooms, destemmed and sliced
1 small red bell pepper, cut into ⅛-inch julienne
1 pound bay scallops
2 tablespoons cognac

½ cup white vermouth
1 cup heavy cream
½ cup peeled and diced ripe tomato
2 tablespoons paper-thin-sliced black truffle
2 tablespoons butter, cut into ½-inch cubes
salt and pepper as needed

- Sauté the shallots and garlic in the olive oil for 5 minutes. Add the mushrooms and bell pepper, and sauté 3 more minutes. Add the scallops, and sauté 1 minute.
- Thoroughly blend in the cognac and vermouth.
- Using a slotted spoon, remove the vegetables and scallops, and set them aside.
- Simmer the remaining liquid until it is reduced by half. Add the heavy cream, and again reduce by half.
- Add the diced tomato and truffles. Add the butter piece by piece, stirring until it is fully incorporated. Return the scallops and vegetables to the pan, and simmer another 3 minutes. Season to taste with salt and pepper.

Wine recommendation: rich chardonnay

Grilled Shrimp Forestière, Cilantro Cream

Four Servings

FOR THE CREAM
1 cup julienned, destemmed shiitake mushrooms
1 cup julienned oyster mushrooms
4 cloves elephant garlic, cut into julienne

2 tablespoons butter
1 cup dry white wine
2 cups heavy cream
salt and pepper as needed
½ cup chopped fresh cilantro

FOR THE PASTA

1 pound dry buckwheat fettucine or other pasta variety

3 tablespoons olive oil
salt and pepper as needed

FOR THE SHRIMP

2 pounds large shrimp (U-12s), peeled and deveined, with tails intact

salt, pepper, and olive oil as needed

TO PREPARE THE CREAM

• Sauté the mushrooms and garlic in the butter for 3 or 4 minutes. Add the white wine. Simmer, and reduce until almost completely dry. Add the cream, and simmer until reduced by half. Season to taste with salt and pepper. Add the chopped cilantro. Set aside.

TO PREPARE THE PASTA

• Bring 2 gallons of lightly salted water to a boil. Add the pasta, and cook 8 to 10 minutes, or until tender but still firm (al dente). Drain, then return to the pot, and add the olive oil, salt, and pepper. Set aside.

TO PREPARE THE SHRIMP

• Prepare an outdoor grill.
• Sprinkle the shrimp with salt and pepper, coat them with the olive oil, and grill them 3 minutes on each side.
• Arrange one-quarter of the pasta into a nest on each of 4 individual serving plates. Place 5 or 6 grilled shrimp on top of each pasta nest, then ladle over the sauce.

Wine recommendation: full-bodied sparkling blanc de blancs

Deveining shrimp is a simple task. After removing the shell, run the blade of a sharp paring knife down the back of the shrimp, scoring about ⅛ inch into the flesh. Then, under cold water, rinse out any impurities that lie in this channel.

Shrimp (or prawn) sizes are indicated by their count per pound. U-10s (giant, or extra colossal), for example, are large shrimp, numbering 10 or fewer to a pound; 10/15s (colossal) are slightly smaller, numbering between 10 and 15 per pound. These are followed by 16/20s (extra jumbo), 21/25s (jumbo), 26/30s (extra large), 31/35s (large), 36/42s (medium large), 43/50s (medium), 51/60s (small), 61/70s (extra small), 70/100s (titi). In Iceland, midgets may run to 150 per pound and, in Holland, to as high as 300, each the length of the nail on your little finger.

Be careful not to overcook the prawns (shrimp). They should be cooked only until they lose their translucence. Overcooked shellfish is tough and rubbery.

POULTRY

Peanut Chicken, Raspberry Vinegar

Four Servings

1 2½- to 3-pound fresh
  roasting chicken, cut into
  8 pieces
salt and pepper as needed
4 tablespoons (½ stick)
  butter
5 shallots, minced

½ cup raspberry vinegar
1 cup Madeira
½ cup blanched raw
  peanuts, broken in half
⅓ cup chopped fresh
  parsley

- Preheat an oven to 350° F.
- Season the chicken lightly with salt and pepper. In a small braising pan, brown it on both sides in the butter. Remove, and set it aside.
- In the same pan, sauté the shallots for 5 minutes. Deglaze with raspberry vinegar and Madeira, add the peanuts, then return the chicken to the pan. Cover, and bake for 45 minutes.
- Remove the chicken once again, and set aside. Simmer the sauce until it is reduced by half. Season to taste with salt and pepper.
- Place the chicken on an appropriate serving platter, pour the sauce over it, and sprinkle it with chopped parsley.

Wine recommendation: spicy gewürztraminer

Breast of Turkey Marsala

Marsala is a slightly sweet wine made from Sicilian grapes. Similar to sweet sherries and Madeira, it is drunk as an aperitif and used in cooking and pastry making.

Four Servings

8 4-ounce turkey breast
  cutlets
salt, pepper, and flour as
  needed
¼ cup vegetable oil
4 tablespoons (½ stick)
  butter
1 medium Spanish onion,
  cut into small dice

2 cups sliced mushrooms
1 garlic clove, minced
juice of ½ lemon
½ cup marsala
¼ cup chopped fresh
  parsley

- Sprinkle the turkey cutlets lightly with salt and pepper, then dust them lightly with flour.
- Heat the vegetable oil in a cast-iron skillet or sauté pan. Sauté the cutlets until they are lightly browned on both sides. Remove, and set aside. Pour off the excess oil from the pan, and discard it.
- Melt the butter in the same pan. Add the onions, and sauté 3 minutes. Add the mushrooms and garlic, and sauté 5 more minutes.
- Deglaze the pan with the lemon juice and marsala. Simmer another 5 minutes. Return the turkey cutlets to the pan, and heat, tossing well with the sauce. Sprinkle with the chopped parsley, and serve.

Wine recommendation: light Beaujolais or Grenache

Breast of Duck
Stuffed with Spinach and Currants

Four Servings

1 pound fresh spinach, stems trimmed, well washed, and roughly chopped
¼ cup dried currants, soaked in ¼ cup warm brandy
¼ cup chicken or duck stock
1 large egg
¾ cup dry bread crumbs
1 teaspoon chopped fresh tarragon leaves
1 tablespoon chopped fresh basil leaves
¼ teaspoon salt
¼ teaspoon pepper
4 boneless duck breast halves, skin on
2 tablespoons clarified unsalted butter
3 tablespoons unsalted butter

- Bring ½ cup of lightly salted water to a boil, add the spinach, and simmer for 3 or 4 minutes. Drain, and squeeze the spinach dry.
- Place the spinach in a bowl, and thoroughly blend in the currants (and the brandy in which they soaked), stock, egg, bread crumbs, herbs, salt, and pepper.
- Preheat an oven to 400° F.
- Cut a pocket in one long side of each breast half, being careful not to cut through any of the other sides.

The species of currant grown commercially is a native of Northern Europe brought to North America during colonial times. In France, black currants, though extremely sour, are grown to produce a popular dessert beverage, cassis, as well as jams and jellies. Red currant jelly, popular in French cookery as a seal for pastry, is also used in Cumberland sauce, a traditional accompaniment to game. Fresh red and white currants can be eaten with cream and sugar, but they are found only occasionally in specialty markets during the summer months. Production has declined in the United States, because the currant is host to a tree fungus, white pine blister rust.

- Stuff each breast half with the stuffing, then close each opening with a toothpick.
- Heat the clarified butter in a cast-iron skillet. Sauté the duck, skin side down, over a medium flame for about 5 minutes, then turn skin side up, and place in the oven to cook for 5 minutes more. Remove from the oven, and allow to rest for 5 minutes. Slice each breast half into 5 pieces, and arrange in a fan shape on an appropriate serving plate.
- Place the remaining butter into the pan, and, over a medium flame, cook it until it turns a hazelnut brown. Pour this over the duck. Serve with a seasonal vegetable and a simple salad.

Wine recommendation: rich Pinot Noir

Roast Quail, Beach Plum Sauce

Four Servings

8 quail	4 tablespoons Dijon
16 strips of bacon	mustard
1 large shallot, minced	1 cup heavy cream
1 tablespoon butter	salt and pepper as needed
½ cup cognac	
1 10-ounce jar beach plum	
or plum jelly	

- Preheat an oven to 400° F.
- Fold the wing tips back under the body of each quail. With the quail lying breast up, make a small incision in the tail end of each bird, just below the cavity opening. Push down on the legs, cross the ends of the drum sticks, and insert them into this incision.
- Wrap each quail in 2 slices of bacon, and secure with a toothpick.
- Place the quail in a roasting pan, and roast for 10 minutes. Turn down the temperature to 375° F, turn over the quail, and continue roasting another 15 to 20 minutes, until the juices run clear when the upper thigh is pierced with a fork. Remove from the oven, and set aside.
- In a small saucepan, sauté the shallot in the butter. Add the cognac, and simmer until almost completely dry. Add the jelly, mustard, and heavy cream, and simmer until reduced by half. Season to taste with salt and pepper. Remove

The beach plum thrives in the very sandy soil found in eastern and northeastern seashore communities in the United States. The plant blossoms in May, and the berries are ready to pick in early October. Ranging in diameter from 1 to 2 inches, depending on the wetness of the summer, at harvest time, the berries are pink on one side and red on the other. Round and smooth like plums —hence their name—the fruit is very juicy, with large pits. Because of their bitterness, beach plums can only be used for jelly, jam, or wine, a Nantucket specialty.

the toothpicks from the quail, and serve accompanied by the sauce.

Wine recommendation: Pinot Noir

VEAL

Roast Loin of Veal with Wild Mushroom Mousse, Madeira Sauce

Six Servings

FOR THE MOUSSE
¼ cup olive oil
½ pound assorted wild mushrooms (chanterelles, morels, cèpes, oyster mushrooms, shiitakes, etc.), roughly chopped
4 ounces very finely ground veal

2 large eggs
pinch salt
pinch pepper
pinch freshly grated nutmeg
1 cup heavy cream
1 tablespoon unsalted butter, softened

FOR THE VEAL
1 2- or 3-pound boneless veal loin, butterflied

olive oil, salt, and pepper as needed

FOR THE SAUCE
2 shallots, minced
2 tablespoons butter

1 cup Madeira
2 cups demi-glace

TO PREPARE THE MOUSSE
• Remove the stems from the mushrooms, and set them aside for use in the sauce.
• Rinse and dry the mushrooms, then sauté in the olive oil for 3 or 4 minutes.
• Transfer the mushrooms to a food processor. Add the remaining mousse ingredients, and puree until smooth.

TO PREPARE THE VEAL
• Preheat an oven to 450° F.
• Spread the mushroom mousse on the butterflied veal loin.

Roll up, and tie with cotton twine or butcher's cord. Rub lightly with olive oil, and sprinkle with salt and pepper.
• Roast the loin for 10 minutes. Turn down the heat to 350° F, and roast for 15 minutes more. Remove from the oven, and set the loin aside on a serving platter.

TO PREPARE THE SAUCE
• Pour the excess oil from the roasting pan, and discard it. Pour the Madeira into the pan, place over a medium flame, and, using a wooden spoon, loosen all caramelized material from the pan. Remove from the fire, and set aside.
• Sauté the shallots and the reserved mushroom stems in the butter for 3 or 4 minutes. Add the Madeira, and simmer until reduced by two-thirds. Add the demi-glace, and simmer until reduced by one-third to one-half, or until the sauce has reached the desired consistency. Strain, and serve over the sliced veal loin.

Wine recommendation: merlot

GAME

Vinegar-braised Rabbit with Red Onion–Apple Chutney and Spaetzle

Four Servings

FOR THE CHUTNEY
1 pound Bermuda onions, thinly sliced
3 Granny Smith apples, peeled, cored, and roughly chopped
¼ cup cider vinegar
1 cup dry red wine
4 tablespoons honey

FOR THE RABBIT
2 whole dressed rabbits, cut into 6 to 8 pieces each
¼ cup olive or vegetable oil
salt and pepper as needed
¼ cup minced shallots
2 garlic cloves, mashed
1 heaping tablespoon flour
1 cup balsamic vinegar
2 cups chicken stock
1 cup chopped fresh herbs (e.g., rosemary, thyme, marjoram, parsley, basil)

FOR THE SPAETZLE
2 large eggs
1 cup water
3 cups flour

pinch salt
pinch pepper
pinch freshly grated nutmeg

FOR SERVING
1 tablespoon butter
salt and pepper as needed

¼ cup poppy seeds

TO PREPARE THE CHUTNEY
- Simmer all of the ingredients over a very low fire in a heavy-gauge saucepan, covered, for 2 hours. Cool, cover, and refrigerate for 24 hours before serving.

TO PREPARE THE RABBIT
- Preheat an oven to 350° F.
- Sprinkle the rabbit pieces lightly with salt and pepper, then brown in the oil in a braising pan. Remove the rabbit, and set aside.
- Using the same pan, sauté the shallots and garlic, then blend in the flour, and cook 3 or 4 minutes. Thoroughly blend in the vinegar, stock, and half of the chopped herbs. Return the rabbit pieces to the pan, cover, and place in the oven for 1 hour.

TO PREPARE THE SPAETZLE
- Beat the eggs and water together. Add the dry ingredients, and beat until thoroughly blended.
- Set a colander over a pot of rapidly boiling, lightly salted water. Spoon in the spaetzle mixture, and use a flexible rubber spatula to press it through. When the water comes back to a boil, drain the spaetzle in a colander, then cool in ice-cold water.

TO SERVE
- Sauté the spaetzle in butter, and season with salt and pepper. Place on an appropriate serving platter, and sprinkle with poppy seeds.
- Place the rabbit on the bed of spaetzle. Adjust the sauce seasoning, add the remaining herbs, and pour the sauce over the rabbit. Serve accompanied by the chutney.

Wine recommendation: Pinot Noir or claret-style zinfandel

Beer-braised Rabbit with Grainy Mustard

Four Servings

½ pound skinless fatback,
  cut into ½-inch cubes
2 dressed rabbits, cut into 8
  pieces each
salt and pepper as needed
2 garlic cloves, minced
2 shallots, minced
2 tablespoons flour
1 12-ounce bottle dark beer
½ cup grainy mustard

2 tablespoons chardonnay
  (or white wine) vinegar
2 cups chicken stock
1 bay leaf
2 sprigs fresh thyme
2 sprigs fresh rosemary
8 slices toasted French
  bread, spread with grainy
  mustard

- Place the fatback in a braising pan large enough to hold all the ingredients, and render over a medium flame until it is dark and crispy. Remove the crispy pieces, and set aside.
- Sprinkle the rabbit pieces lightly with salt and pepper, and brown well in the rendered fat. Add the garlic and shallots, and sauté 3 minutes.
- Blend in the flour thoroughly, and cook for 5 minutes.
- Stir in the beer, then the mustard, vinegar, stock, bay leaf, thyme, rosemary, and fatback pieces. Cover, and simmer for 1 hour, or until the rabbit meat is very tender.
- Serve on top of the toasted French bread.

Wine recommendation: merlot

Final Courses

COLD DESSERTS

Fresh Figs with Chestnut and Cranberry Mousse

Four Servings

Heated in a 350° F oven for 10 or 15 minutes, this same dish can be served as a garnish for game.

3 tablespoons water	2 cups chestnut puree
1 cup whole fresh (or fresh-frozen) cranberries	¼ cup heavy cream
	pinch freshly grated nutmeg
⅓ cup granulated sugar	20 small fresh figs

- Combine the water, cranberries, and sugar in a small saucepan. Bring to a boil, and simmer for 4 minutes. (The cranberries should *not* open up.) Remove from the fire.
- Process two-thirds of the cranberry mixture with the chestnut puree and nutmeg in a blender, adding the cream in a slow steady stream.
- Cut the figs in half horizontally. Fill a pastry bag fitted with a large (No. 2) round tip. Pipe a small amount of the mousse onto half of the fig halves. Cap each half with its mate, slightly askew, so that the mousse can be seen. Place a heaping teaspoon of the remaining cranberry mixture on the mousse. Chill and serve.

Blackberry and Scotch Cheesecake

Ten to Twelve Servings

FOR THE CRUST
1¼ cups flour, sifted
¼ cup granulated sugar
8 tablespoons (1 stick)
   unsalted butter, cut into
   ¼-inch cubes

FOR THE FILLING
19 ounces cream cheese
1 teaspoon vanilla extract
2½ tablespoons Drambuie
½ teaspoon ground
   cinnamon
¾ cup granulated sugar

3 large eggs
juice and grated rind of
   1 lemon
½ pound dry-packed frozen
   blackberries, not thawed

FOR THE TOPPING
2 cups sour cream
1 tablespoon granulated
   sugar

1 teaspoon vanilla extract

TO PREPARE THE CRUST
• Preheat an oven to 375° F.
• Combine the sugar, flour, and butter, rubbing the mixture together between your palms until it resembles coarse meal. Press the dough into the bottom of a buttered 9-inch springform pan. Bake for 25 minutes. Allow to cool.

TO PREPARE THE FILLING
• Preheat oven to 375° F.
• Beat the cream cheese in a bowl with a hand electric mixer until it is soft and smooth.
• Add the vanilla, Drambuie, cinnamon, and sugar, and continue beating until smooth.
• Add the eggs one at a time, beating each until it is incorporated. Blend in the juice and zest.
• Pour the filling into the baked crust. Top with an even layer of frozen blackberries, gently pressing the berries down into the batter to immerse them.
• Bake for 40 minutes. Allow to stand at room temperature for 20 minutes.

TO PREPARE THE TOPPING
- Thoroughly blend together the sour cream, sugar, and vanilla, and pour this on top of the cake. Bake for 5 minutes. Allow to cool to room temperature, then refrigerate overnight.

WARM DESSERTS

Cherry Cobbler

Twelve Servings

FOR THE FILLING
⅓ cup flour
pinch salt
¼ teaspoon ground allspice
¼ teaspoon ground cinnamon
⅓ cup granulated sugar
2 cups cherry juice

2 tablespoons lemon juice
2 pounds fresh ripe Bing cherries, rinsed and pitted
10 tablespoons (1¼ sticks) unsalted butter, cut into ½-inch cubes

FOR THE DOUGH
1 cup flour
1 teaspoon baking powder
¼ teaspoon baking soda
¼ teaspoon salt

2½ tablespoons cold unsalted butter, cut into ¼-inch cubes
⅓ cup cold buttermilk

FOR ASSEMBLY
1 egg, beaten

powdered sugar as needed

TO PREPARE THE FILLING
- Sift the dry ingredients together. Whisk them into the cherry juice until the mixture is smooth. Place in a saucepan with the lemon juice and cherries, bring to a boil, and simmer for 2 minutes, stirring continuously. Remove from the fire, and stir in the butter until it is fully incorporated. Set aside.

TO PREPARE THE DOUGH
- Sift the dry ingredients together. Add the butter, and rub the mixture together between your palms until it resembles

Use a standard No. 2 pencil with the eraser removed to pit fresh cherries. Simply push the small cylindrical cavity at the end of the pencil through the center of each cherry.

If bottled cherry juice is not available, substitute another variety, such as grape or apple.

Other varieties or combinations of fruit can be used in this dish to fit the season. The chef suggests blueberry-peach, huckleberry-pear, raspberry-pear, and so on.

A deep-dish fruit pie, made with a top crust of short dough, with or without a bottom crust is known by many different names. Cobbler, a name used in the South and southern midwestern states, is made with a top crust of biscuit dough, in a single solid layer or formed into individual biscuits or "cobbles." A crisp or brown betty is often made of apples or blueberries, baked with a top layer of buttered crumbs, sometimes mixed with nuts. A crumble is an English cousin to our crisp, often made of rhubarb or gooseberries topped with a crunchy shortbread made of oats, flour, butter, and brown sugar. A pandowdy is generally made of sliced apples baked with a bread-dough crust that is cut up and pressed back into the fruit during the last few minutes of baking. "Dowdying" may be an old New England colloquialism for cutting up dough. A buckle consists of berries folded into or sprinkled over a yellow cake batter, then baked and cut into squares. A grunt or slump is similar to a cobbler, but it is steamed on top of the stove, often in a cast-iron skillet.

coarse meal. Add the buttermilk, and stir just until it is incorporated. Do not overmix.
- Roll out the dough on a floured surface to a thickness of ⅜ inch.

TO ASSEMBLE
- Preheat an oven to 400° F.
- Lightly butter a 2-quart ovenproof casserole dish. Pour in the filling. Cut the dough to fit the top, and set it into place. Brush the dough lightly with the beaten egg, and bake for 15 minutes, or until golden brown. Sprinkle with powdered sugar.

Poached Apples, Caramel Sauce

Four Servings

FOR THE SAUCE

¾ cup granulated sugar
3 tablespoons water

1 tablespoon lemon juice
¼ cup warm heavy cream

FOR THE APPLES

4 cups water
juice of 1 lemon
½ cup granulated sugar

2 whole cloves
4 Granny Smith apples,
    peeled and cored

TO PREPARE THE SAUCE
- Simmer the sugar, water, and lemon juice in a small saucepan, stirring continuously, until the mixture begins to turn a light brown. Add the cream, and remove the sauce from the fire immediately. Stir until smooth. Set aside.

TO PREPARE THE APPLES
- Combine all of the ingredients in a saucepan. Bring the mixture to a boil, and simmer for approximately 15 minutes, or until the apples are tender but still very firm. Remove from the fire, and drain.
- Place the apples on individual serving plates, fill their centers with chocolate ice cream (optional), and top with the warmed caramel sauce.

Crêpes Suzette

Four to Five Servings

FOR THE CRÊPES
2 large eggs
¾ cup flour
pinch salt

1 cup milk
2 tablespoons melted
    unsalted butter

FOR THE SAUCE
⅓ cup granulated sugar
4 tablespoons (½ stick)
    unsalted butter
juice and zest of 2 oranges

juice and zest of 1 lemon
⅓ cup Grand Marnier
⅓ cup cognac

TO PREPARE THE CRÊPES
• Whip the eggs, flour, and salt in a mixing bowl until smooth. Add the milk and butter, and again blend until smooth. Allow to rest for 2 hours.
• Lightly butter a 6- or 7-inch nonstick sauté pan. Heat over a low flame. Pour approximately ¼ cup of the batter into the pan. When the top of the crêpe is dry, turn the crêpe over, cook for another 30 seconds, then remove. Repeat this procedure until all the batter has been used. The recipe should yield 12 to 15 crêpes.

TO PREPARE THE SAUCE
• Lightly caramelize the sugar and butter in a sauté pan. Blend in the juices and zest, add the Grand Marnier, and bring to a boil. Place the crêpes in the sauce one at a time, folding each into quarters before adding the rest. Remove from the fire, add the cognac, and flame. Serve 3 crêpes per person.

The 95th Cranberry Fritters, Raspberry Sauce

Four to Six Servings

FOR THE SAUCE
1 pint fresh raspberries
½ cup granulated sugar

¼ cup Cherry Heering, or
    other sweet fruit liqueur

Henri Charpentier operated several restaurants in the New York City area during the early part of this century. He is the author of a charming autobiography, Life à la Henri, *published in 1934 and illustrated with black-and-white photographs by Margaret Bourke-White. The following is excerpted from his book:*

"It was 1894, and I, at the tender age of 14 years, was holding the position of commis des rangs [waiter] at the Café de Paris in Monte Carlo. Queen Victoria's son Edward, the Prince of Wales, came in for lunch one day. 'Bonjour, Henri,' said the Prince gaily. 'What are we going to have for lunch today?' 'Sir, today it will be a sweet never before served to anyone.' [Description of the preparation.] 'He ate the pancakes [crêpes] with a fork; but he used a spoon to capture the remaining syrup. He asked me the name of that which he had eaten with so much relish. I told him it was to be called Crêpes Princesse. He recognized the gender was controlled by the pancake and that this was a compliment designed for him; but he protested with mock ferocity that there was a lady present. She was alert and rose to her feet. Holding her little skirt wide with her hands, she made him a curtsy. 'Will you,' said His Majesty, 'change Crêpes Princesse to Crêpes Suzette?' Thus was born and baptized this confection, one taste of which, I really believe, would reform a cannibal into a civilized gentleman."

The 95th is located on the top (ninety-fifth) floor of the John Hancock Center in Chicago, Illinois. For brunch, lunch, and dinner reservations, telephone (315) 787-9596.

FOR THE FRITTERS

¼ cup water

¼ cup plus 3 tablespoons granulated sugar

1½ cups whole fresh (or fresh-frozen) cranberries

3 eggs, separated

1 cup milk

½ tablespoon vegetable oil

½ tablespoon lemon juice

1½ cups flour

1½ teaspoons baking powder

¼ teaspoon salt

vegetable oil as needed

powdered sugar as needed

TO PREPARE THE SAUCE

- Sprinkle the berries with the sugar, and allow them to sit at room temperature for 1 hour.
- Puree the berries and sugar, along with the liqueur, in a food processor.
- Press the puree through a sieve, discard the seeds, then set the sauce aside.

TO PREPARE THE FRITTERS

- Preheat an oven to 200° F.
- Combine the water, ¼ cup sugar, and cranberries in a small saucepan. Bring to a boil, then simmer for 5 to 8 minutes, or until syrupy. Cool.
- Beat together the egg yolks, milk, vegetable oil, lemon juice, and 3 tablespoons sugar. In a separate bowl, beat the egg whites until they form stiff peaks.
- Combine the flour, baking powder, and salt, and sprinkle this mixture slowly into the liquid mixture, stirring continuously. Add the cranberries, and fold in the egg whites.
- Heat 3 inches of vegetable oil to 365° F in a heavy-gauge pan. Drop the batter by heaping tablespoonfuls into the oil. Fry until the fritters are golden brown on both sides. When done, transfer them to absorbent paper, and keep them warm in the oven until ready to serve.

PIES

Sweet Potato–Pecan Pie

Eight to Ten Servings

FOR THE CRUST
1⅛ cups flour
¼ teaspoon salt
6 tablespoons (¾ stick)
   unsalted butter, cut into
   ¼-inch cubes

2 tablespoons cold water

FOR THE FILLING
3 tablespoons unsalted
   butter, softened
3½ tablespoons granulated
   sugar
¼ cup dark brown sugar

1 teaspoon vanilla extract
1 cup dark corn syrup
1 cup pureed sweet potatoes
6 large eggs
1¾ cups pecan pieces

Pie crust is a short dough, so named for its use of "shortening," some form of fat—usually butter and/or lard—that effectively shortens the gluten strands in the flour. Gluten is an element that develops in flour when it is mixed with liquid and then kneaded. Breads have little or no fat in them and are kneaded vigorously to develop the gluten, in order to produce a strong, chewy product. Biscuits, butter cookies, and pie dough have greater proportions of fat—shortening—and require minimal handling so that the end product will be light and flaky.

TO PREPARE THE CRUST
- Sift the flour and salt into a mixing bowl. Add the cubed butter, then rub the mixture together between your palms, until it resembles coarse meal.
- Add the water, then press the dough together, kneading as little as possible, to form one large ball. Wrap this in plastic, and refrigerate for ½ hour.
- Roll out the dough on a lightly floured board to a thickness of approximately ⅛ inch. Fold it in half, then gently lift it, and place it into an 8- or 9-inch round glass pie dish. Press the dough into the dish, trim and crimp the edges, then pierce the dough all over with a fork.

TO PREPARE THE FILLING
- Preheat an oven to 350° F.
- With a hand electric mixer, cream the butter, sugars, and vanilla together in a mixing bowl until the sugars are completely dissolved.
- Still beating, add the corn syrup and the sweet potatoes until they are fully blended. Add the eggs, one at a time, beating each until it is fully incorporated before adding the next. Stir in the pecan pieces.

- Pour the filling into the pie shell, and bake for 40 to 45 minutes, or until it is set.

CAKES AND BREADS

Pennsylvania Dutch Apple Cake

Eight to Ten Servings

2 large Granny Smith apples	¼ cup milk
½ cup granulated sugar	pinch salt
1 teaspoon ground cinnamon	⅓ cup flour
3 large eggs	2 tablespoons unsalted butter

- Peel, core, and quarter the apples, then cut the quarters into very fine wedges, ⅛ inch thick.
- Combine the sugar with the cinnamon. Place the apples in a bowl, and toss them with half of the sugar and cinnamon. Set aside.
- Beat the eggs and milk together in a small bowl until they are light and frothy. Whip in the salt and flour until the batter is smooth.
- Preheat an oven to 400° F.
- Melt the butter in a 9-inch cast-iron skillet. Sauté the apple slices 30 seconds. Cool briefly, then arrange the apples in two concentric circles in the skillet.
- Pour in the batter, and cook over a low flame for 2 or 3 minutes. Bake for 5 to 8 minutes.
- Invert the skillet over a serving platter, and sprinkle the cake with the remaining sugar and cinnamon.

WINTER

First Courses

COLD APPETIZERS

Gravlax and Asparagus

Four Servings

The practice of dry curing meat and fish with salt is several thousand years old. The salt acts as a dehydrator, drawing out moisture, and a sterilizer, deactivating bacteria. The other elements of the cure—salt, herbs, and spices—add additional flavor and character. Ham, bacon, prosciutto, and corned beef are examples of foods that traditionally are dry cured. Smoking adds further preserving and flavor.

Gravlax is a Scandinavian dish, valued by culinary professionals not as much for its shelf life as for the unique, translucent quality of the fish.

FOR THE GRAVLAX
2 cups kosher salt
¾ cup granulated sugar
3 tablespoons crushed white peppercorns
1 2- to 3-pound fillet of fresh salmon, skin on

¼ cup cognac or brandy
½ cup minced mixed fresh chervil, tarragon, fennel, and dill

FOR THE SAUCE
juice of 2 lemons
6 tablespoons olive oil
6 tablespoons vegetable oil
1 shallot, minced
pinch salt

pinch pepper
1 teaspoon minced fresh parsley
1 teaspoon minced fresh tarragon

FOR SERVING
32 spears medium asparagus, cut into 6-inch lengths
4 tablespoons sturgeon caviar

4 teaspoons capers
4 tablespoons finely diced Bermuda onion
4 tablespoons grated radish
12 small slices of rye bread

TO PREPARE THE GRAVLAX
- Combine the salt, sugar, and peppercorns. Sprinkle a thin layer of this mixture on the bottom of a stainless steel or

glass baking dish large enough to hold the salmon fillet. Place the fillet, skin side down, on the seasoning.
- Rub half of the cognac onto the salmon flesh. Cover with the rest of the seasoning mix, then drizzle the remaining cognac on top. Cover with a sheet of plastic wrap. Place a board roughly the size of the salmon on top of the fish, then press down gently. Weight down the board with several stones. Refrigerate for 24 hours.
- After 24 hours, brush off some of the seasoning mix, leaving only a light layer. Press the chopped herbs onto the salmon, then cover it again with plastic and the weighted board, and return it to the refrigerator to cure for 3 days.
- After 3 days, rinse the salmon very gently, wrap it in plastic, and refrigerate until ready to serve.

TO PREPARE THE SAUCE
- Puree the ingredients in a blender. Refrigerate until ready to serve.

TO SERVE
- Blanch the asparagus in lightly salted boiling water until it is tender but still firm. Drain, cool, and dry.
- Slice the salmon at a very sharp angle, into 32 very thin pieces. Wrap a slice of gravlax around the center of each asparagus. Place 8 wrapped asparagus on each of 4 serving plates. Top each serving with 2 or 3 tablespoons of sauce, and garnish with caviar, capers, onion, radish, and the bread.

Wine recommendation: champagne or sparkling chardonnay

Chicken Breasts Stuffed with Cranberry Mousse

Four Servings

FOR THE SAUCE

1 cup cranberry juice	1 teaspoon minced orange zest
¼ cup Grand Marnier	
½ cup whole fresh (or fresh-frozen) cranberries	1 tablespoon granulated sugar

FOR THE CHICKEN

10 ounces chicken breast meat, cut into ½-inch cubes

1 tablespoon Grand Marnier

½ teaspoon salt

¼ teaspoon white pepper

¼ cup heavy cream

¼ cup whole fresh (or fresh-frozen) cranberries

4 4-ounce boneless, skinless chicken breast halves

FOR SERVING

16 skinless, seedless orange segments

8 fresh mint leaves

TO PREPARE THE SAUCE

- Combine all the ingredients in a saucepan. Bring to a boil, and simmer for 3 minutes. Puree in a blender, push through a fine sieve, cover, and refrigerate.

TO PREPARE THE CHICKEN

- Place the diced chicken meat in the freezer for 1 hour. Combine in a food processor with the Grand Marnier, salt, and pepper, and puree.
- Pour in the cream, and continue to puree.
- Fold in the cranberries, then set aside.
- Cut a pocket in the long side of each chicken breast, being careful not to cut through to the other sides.
- Fill a pastry bag with the mousse, then pipe the mousse into the pockets cut into the breasts. Wrap each filled breast tightly in plastic wrap. Place the breasts in a steamer basket, then place the basket in a saucepan. Pour about an inch of water into the pan, cover, and steam for 8 minutes. Remove the chicken from the steamer, and refrigerate it, still wrapped, until well chilled.

TO SERVE

- Pour ¼ cup of the chilled sauce on each of 4 serving plates. Slice the chicken breasts across their widths, and arrange the slices over the sauce. Garnish each serving with 4 orange segments and 2 mint leaves.

Wine recommendation: Beaujolais

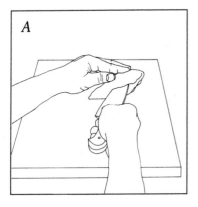

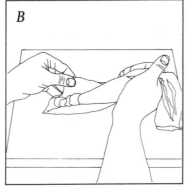

Slice a pocket into each chicken breast (A). Stuff each breast with the cranberry mousse (B). Wrap the breasts in plastic wrap (C).

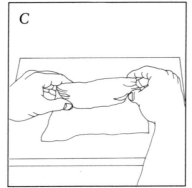

HOT APPETIZERS

Crab Cakes, Jalapeño Sauce

Four Servings

FOR THE SAUCE

1 large Spanish onion, peeled and roughly chopped
2 garlic cloves
2 jalapeño peppers, split, ribs and seeds discarded

3 green bell peppers, split, ribs and seeds discarded
2 tablespoons olive oil
1 cup white wine
1 cup cream
¼ teaspoon salt

Hot peppers include anaheims, sometimes known as New Mexico peppers, Rio Grande peppers, or California peppers, which are 6 to 8 inches long, slender, green, and relatively mild, and used for making chiles rellenos, a fried, cheese-stuffed dish, and ground for chili powder and paprika when mature; anchos, the correct name for the ripened and dried poblano, 5 inches long and dark brick red, the most commonly used chili in Mexico; cayenne peppers, chiles de arbol, Thai peppers, all sometimes known as "bird peppers" in Asian markets, while not exactly the same, are similar—small, thin peppers, found green, red, and dried, the fresh red variety being hotter than the green; cherry peppers, small, round, red or green peppers, often pickled, and available in most supermarkets; jalapeños, about 2 inches long, smooth skinned, and green, often pickled; pasillas, 6 inches long, narrow, with wide shoulders, dark green or nearly black when fresh and dark brown when dried, moderately hot with a deep rich flavor; pepperoncinis, small, moderately hot, light green peppers, packed in vinegar, often found in Italian and Greek markets; poblanos, also known as anchos, ranging from 2½ to 6 inches in length, dark green to nearly black, wide at the shoulder, and tapered to a point at the bottom; serranos, slender, very hot green chilies, about 2 inches long, used raw and pickled; and yellow wax peppers, about 5 inches long, also known as Hungarian wax peppers.

FOR THE CRAB CAKES

¼ cup minced shallots
4 tablespoons (½ stick) butter
¼ cup Pernod
1 tablespoon butter, softened
1½ tablespoons flour
½ cup crème fraîche or sour cream

½ teaspoon salt
¼ teaspoon white pepper
1 pound Dungeness crabmeat, shredded
4 large eggs, lightly beaten
4 cups fresh white bread crumbs
vegetable oil as needed

FOR SERVING

8 lemon wedges

4 sprigs fresh dill

TO PREPARE THE SAUCE

- Sauté the onion, garlic, and peppers in the olive oil. Add the white wine, and simmer 5 minutes. Add the cream and salt, and simmer another few minutes. Puree in a food processor, and set aside.

TO PREPARE THE CRAB CAKES

- Sauté the shallots in the 4 tablespoons of butter for 5 minutes. Add the Pernod, and cook another 3 minutes. Mix the softened butter with the flour, and stir the paste thoroughly into the shallots. Cook for 3 or 4 minutes, then allow to cool for a few minutes.
- Add the crème fraîche, salt, pepper, crabmeat, and eggs to the shallots. Blend thoroughly.
- Shape the crab mixture into 8 oval-shaped patties. Roll these in the bread crumbs, pressing the crumbs firmly into each patty. Cover and refrigerate for 1 hour.
- Preheat an oven to 300° F.
- Pour 1 inch of vegetable oil into a heavy-gauge pot, and heat to a temperature of 365° F. Fry the crab cakes until golden brown on each side. Transfer to absorbent paper, and place in the warm oven until ready to serve.

TO SERVE

- Serve 2 cakes per person, garnished with lemon wedges, dill, and a side of the jalapeño sauce.

Wine recommendation: Riesling

Ocean Sausages with Salmon Caviar, Parsley Sauce

Four Servings

FOR THE SAUSAGE

6 ounces skinless salmon fillet, cut into ½-inch pieces

6 ounces boneless, skinless snapper, cut into ½-inch pieces

½ pound fresh sea scallops

2 teaspoons chopped fresh dill

1 teaspoon chopped fresh tarragon

1 teaspoon chopped fresh parsley

½ teaspoon salt

¼ teaspoon freshly ground white pepper

½ cup dry white wine

24 inches sheep sausage casing

FOR THE SAUCE

1 bunch fresh parsley, stems removed

1½ cups heavy cream

½ cup fish stock

½ cup dry white wine

salt and pepper to taste

FOR SERVING

2 tablespoons vegetable oil

2 tablespoons salmon caviar

TO PREPARE THE SAUSAGE

- Place the fish in the freezer for 30 minutes, then puree in a food processor, along with the herbs, salt, pepper, and wine.
- Fit a pastry bag with a round-holed tube, and fill it with the puree. Slide one end of the sausage casings over the tube, and carefully pipe the puree into the casings. When they are filled, twist them at approximately 4-inch intervals.

TO PREPARE THE SAUCE

- Blanch the parsley in boiling salted water for 3 minutes. Drain, and puree in a food processor with a little of the cream.
- Simmer the stock and wine in a small saucepan until it is reduced by two-thirds. Add the remaining cream, and simmer until reduced by half. Stir in the parsley puree, and season to taste with salt and pepper.

Commercially prepared sausage is filled mechanically, using a funnel-like attachment on a meat grinder. The casings are slipped over the tip of this attachment, and the farce—the ground meat or fish—is pushed into them.

Another way of preparing the sausage in this recipe is simply to wrap small portions of the farce in small sheets of pig's caul, skin that comes from the belly of a sow. (See Duck Breasts and Sausages, Rhubarb Compote, Summer, Main Courses, page 81.)

TO SERVE
- Sauté the sausages in the oil over a low flame until they are fully cooked (about 4 minutes on each side). Separate the sausages, and serve 2 per person, topped with the sauce and garnished with the caviar.

Wine recommendation: champagne or sparkling chardonnay

Rouille—literally "rust"—is a garlic-flavored, crimson-colored mayonnaise. Spread on toasted French bread slices, it is the traditional accompaniment to bouillabaisse, a hearty Mediterranean fish stew.

Deviled Crab Sausages, Sweet Pepper Sauce

Four Servings

FOR THE SAUCE

4 medium red bell peppers
olive oil as needed
1 medium Spanish onion, roughly chopped
3 tablespoons butter

1 garlic clove, minced
1 small red jalapeño pepper, split, seeded, and minced
1½ cups chicken stock
salt and pepper to taste

FOR THE ROUILLE

1 large egg yolk
juice of 1 lemon
pinch salt
¼ teaspoon cayenne pepper

¾ teaspoon paprika
1 garlic clove, minced
1 cup olive oil

FOR THE SAUSAGES

3 ounces scallops
3 ounces rockfish (snapper)
½ teaspoon salt
½ cup heavy cream
1 small garlic clove, minced
1 teaspoon dry mustard
1 teaspoon cayenne pepper
½ teaspoon paprika
1 teaspoon grated fresh ginger root
1 tablespoon chopped fresh cilantro

1 tablespoon chopped fresh basil
1 tablespoon chopped fresh parsley
12 ounces crabmeat
8 pieces pork caul, approximately 5 by 5 inches
butter as needed

TO PREPARE THE SAUCE
- Preheat an oven to 400° F.
- Rub the peppers with olive oil, place on a baking sheet, and roast until nearly completely black. Remove from the oven, place in a bowl, and cover tightly with plastic wrap.

- After 10 minutes, remove the peppers from the bowl. Tear them open, and separate the flesh from the skin and seeds.
- Sauté the onion in the butter for 5 minutes. Add the garlic and jalapeño pepper, and sauté another couple of minutes. Add the chicken stock, and simmer until reduced by one third. Puree the sautéed ingredients and the roasted peppers in a food processor, return to the fire, and simmer until reduced to the desired thickness. Season to taste with salt and pepper, and set aside.

TO PREPARE THE ROUILLE
- Whisk all of the ingredients except for the olive oil in a small bowl. Then, whisking continuously, pour in the olive oil in a slow steady stream until it is completely emulsified. Set aside.

TO PREPARE THE SAUSAGES
- Place the scallops and rockfish in the freezer for 30 minutes. Puree in a food processor with the salt, then add the cream slowly, continuing to puree. Thoroughly blend in the garlic, mustard, cayenne, paprika, ginger, and herbs. Remove to a bowl, and stir in the crabmeat. Refrigerate for ½ hour.
- Divide the farce into 8 individual patties, and wrap each in a piece of caul. Sauté in the butter over a low flame, until golden brown on both sides. Serve with the pepper sauce and a side of the rouille.

Wine recommendation: dry Riesling or lean chardonnay

Scallops with Leeks and Endive

Four Servings

2 leeks, white part only, cut into ⅛-inch julienne, well rinsed	12 ounces sea scallops
	½ cup heavy cream
	salt and pepper as needed
3 Belgian endives, trimmed of root ends and cut lengthwise into quarters	2 teaspoons minced fresh chives
2 tablespoons unsalted butter	

- Sauté the leeks and endive in the butter for 3 or 4 minutes. Add the scallops, and sauté for 2 more minutes. Remove

For more than two thousand years, the village of Roquefort sur-Soulzon in the south of France has produced a blue-veined cheese known the world over. The French are proud of their Roquefort cheese, and rightfully so. Its distinctiveness is the result of the patient and time-honored method of its production—a unique combination of nature, geography, and man. Made from the milk of hardy Lacaune sheep, the cheese is cured in 25 naturally occurring caves occupying an area of more than 125 acres of subterranean land and connected by nearly four miles of corridors. But Roquefort is not the only blue-veined cheese in the world.

In this country, the name Maytag is usually associated with washing machines—the company has been manufacturing them since the early 1900s. In the early 1920s, however, Elmer Maytag, son of the founder of the company, began a dairy division as a hobby. In the late 1930s, his son Frederick expanded the dairy division to include the production of a blue cheese using a process innovated and patented by the University of Iowa. Commercial production began in 1941 (when, incidentally, the price of milk in Iowa was ten cents a quart), and the painstaking manual process first employed is still used today.

the scallops and vegetables with a slotted or perforated spoon, and set aside, keeping them warm.
- Add the cream to the pan, and simmer until reduced by half. Return the leeks and endive to the sauce, and simmer another few minutes. Then return the scallops, season to taste with salt and pepper, and simmer another minute.
- Place a portion of the leeks and endive in the center of a serving plate. Place some of the scallops on top, and sprinkle with the chopped chives.

Wine recommendation: dry Riesling

Iowa Blue Cheese Tart

Five Servings

FOR THE CRUST

1 cup flour	1 large egg yolk
½ teaspoon salt	¼ cup ice water
6 tablespoons (¾ stick) unsalted butter, cut into ½-inch cubes	

FOR THE FILLING

2 tablespoons unsalted butter, softened	2 large eggs
pinch salt	4 ounces Maytag Iowa Blue Cheese, crumbled
pinch cayenne pepper	1 cup heavy cream

TO PREPARE THE CRUST

- Rub the flour, salt, and butter together between your palms until the mixture resembles coarse meal. Add the yolk and water, and press the dough into a ball (use a small amount of additional cold water, if necessary). Wrap, and refrigerate for 1 hour.
- Preheat an oven to 400° F.
- Roll out the dough on a floured surface to a thickness of ¹⁄₁₆ inch.
- Lightly butter 5 5-inch round tart pans. Cut out 5 6-inch squares of dough, and press a square into each pan. Trim the dough even with the edge of each pan, then press it gently up the sides of the pan to form a shallow rim. Poke the bottom of each shell several times with the tines of a fork.

- Bake the tart shells for 10 minutes.

TO PREPARE THE FILLING
- Using a hand electric mixer, beat the butter, salt, cayenne, and eggs in a small bowl until smooth and creamy. Thoroughly blend in the crumbled blue cheese and the cream.
- Fill the tart shells three-quarters full with the cheese mixture. Bake for 10 minutes, still at 400° F.

Wine recommendation: high-acid sauvignon blanc

Tillamook Cheese Croquettes, Cilantro Sauce

Four Servings

FOR THE CROQUETTES
1 quart milk	½ pound Tillamook cheddar cheese, shredded
1 whole clove	flour as needed
1 bay leaf	4 large eggs, beaten
½ small onion	4 cups fresh white bread crumbs
4 tablespoons (½ stick) butter	vegetable oil as needed
⅓ cup flour	

FOR THE SAUCE
1 shallot, minced	1 bay leaf
½ jalapeño pepper, split and seeded	1 teaspoon chopped fresh parsley
1 tablespoon butter	½ cup chopped fresh cilantro
4 medium ripe tomatoes, peeled and cored	¼ teaspoon salt
2 tablespoons tomato paste	

FOR SERVING
4 sprigs parsley

TO PREPARE THE CROQUETTES
- Bring the milk, clove, bay leaf, and onion to a simmer. Remove from the fire, and set aside.
- In a heavy-gauge saucepan, melt the butter. Blend in the flour, and cook over a medium flame for 6 to 8 minutes, stirring continuously. Do not brown.
- Strain the milk into the flour-butter mixture, and stir until

Unlike French Roquefort, which is made from sheep's milk, Maytag Iowa Blue is made from the milk of a specially developed herd of black-and-white Holstein-Frisian cows, which graze on sixteen hundred acres of pasturage spread out over five farms in Iowa. Maytag Blue is aged for six months, which accounts in part for its assertive, piquant flavor and soft, crumbly texture.

The rich farmland of Tillamook County, Oregon, is known for its abundance of exceptionally rich milk. From this is made an acclaimed cheddar cheese, unique in that, as it ages, it becomes soft and smooth, instead of dry and crumbly, like other cheddars. Today, Tillamook cheddar is still made from raw milk, just as it was at the end of the nineteenth century.

thick and smooth. Simmer, stirring continuously, for another 10 minutes.
- Thoroughly blend in the cheese, and remove from the fire.
- Pour the mixture into a buttered 9-inch square pan (or another pan of similar dimensions). Cover, and refrigerate 1 hour, or until firm.
- Cut the cheese block into 9 3-inch squares, then cut each square in half diagonally. Dust each triangle with flour, dip in the beaten egg, allowing excess to drip off, then coat with bread crumbs.
- Preheat an oven to 200° F.
- Pour 3 inches of vegetable oil into a heavy-gauge pot, and heat it to 350° F. (Use a candy thermometer to determine the temperature). Gently place some of the triangles into the hot fat—do not crowd them—and fry until golden brown.
- Place on absorbent paper, and keep warm in oven until all the triangles are fried.

TO PREPARE THE SAUCE
- Sauté the shallot and pepper in the butter for 4 or 5 minutes. Add the tomatoes, paste, and bay leaf, and simmer for 30 minutes.
- Remove the bay leaf, and discard it. Puree the sauce in a blender along with the parsley, cilantro, and salt. Reheat when ready to serve.

TO SERVE
- Put 2 or 3 tablespoons of the sauce on 4 individual plates, top with the croquettes, and garnish with parsley.

Wine recommendation: herbaceous sauvignon blanc

Cheese Fondue

Four Servings

1 garlic clove
2 cups dry white wine
2 tablespoons kirsch
8 ounces Emmenthaler
  cheese, grated
8 ounces Gruyère cheese,
  grated
pinch nutmeg
pinch ground cloves

pinch salt
pinch pepper
½ cup Westphalian ham,
  cut into small dice
4 scallions, minced
1 large loaf fresh French
  bread, cut into 1-inch
  cubes

- Rub the garlic clove vigorously all over the inside surface of an earthenware fondue pot.
- Pour the wine and kirsch into the pot, cover, and place on a fondue stand, with the burner lit.
- When the wine and kirsch are very hot, add the cheese. Stir continuously, until the cheese is fully melted, then add the seasonings, ham, and scallions. Serve with the baguette cubes, and provide long forks with which to spear cubes of bread to dip into the hot fondue.

Wine recommendation: dry Riesling

Fondue is a noun form of the French verb fondre, *meaning "to dissolve or melt." It is most commonly associated with a cheese sauce that originated in Switzerland, although, technically speaking, it can also refer to numerous vegetable purees used in a great many dishes. There is also a dessert fondue, a piping hot dish of chocolate, kirsch, cream, and brandy, into which cut fruit and pound cake are dipped, then eaten.*

Fresh Mozzarella and Sun-dried Tomato Pizza

Four Servings

1 cup warm water (110° F)
1 ounce dry yeast
1 tablespoon olive oil
2 cups flour
pinch salt
½ cup sun-dried tomatoes,
  firmly packed
½ cup hot water

⅓ pound fresh mozzarella
  cheese, shredded
2 tablespoons chopped fresh
  basil
1 tablespoon chopped fresh
  oregano leaves
¼ cup olive oil

- Combine the water and the yeast in a bowl, and stir until the yeast is dissolved. Let sit for 5 minutes. Add the tablespoon of oil, 1 cup of the flour, and the salt. Blend thoroughly. Add the remaining flour, and knead into a soft,

The name pizza *may derive from the Neapolitan pronunciation of the Greek word for flat breads,* pincea, *or it may be related to the Latin* pinsere, *meaning to beat or knead. Though it is generally agreed that pizza was invented in Naples, the story of its creation is as varied as are types of pizza fillings. Some credit Rafaele Esposito, a native Neapolitan, with creating the original pizza for Italy's Queen Margherita in 1889. She was reportedly pleased with the offering—embellished with tomato, basil, and mozzarella, in the colors of the Italian flag.*

Quahogs (pronounced cwō-hogs), cherrystones, and littlenecks are all the same bivalve mollusk, named differently to distinguish their size. Anything up to 2¼ inches across its shell is termed a littleneck, anything up to 3 inches across is considered a cherrystone, and anything up to 5 inches across is a quahog. The smaller the clam, the more tender the meat.

Bivalves, which include mussels, oysters, and scallops, are part of a family of invertebrates, their soft bodies supported by an exterior skeleton composed chiefly of calcium. Concentric ridges on the outer shell are evidence of growth.

The word chowder *derives from* chaudière, *the French term for a large, heavy soup pot (chaud means "hot"). French immigrants brought such* chaudières *with them to New England, and their rich soups and stews, such as* bouillabaisse *and* bourride, *eventually came to be called chowders, after the pots in which they were cooked.*

A true New England chowder is the topic of much debate among cooks. The recipe here is fairly close to one published in 1935 in The Boston Cooking School Cookbook, *which was served with "common crackers," similar to what we know as water biscuits. The only differences are the addition of celery and parsley and the substitution of heavy cream for milk and water instead of fish stock to steam the clams.*

smooth dough. Place in a large bowl, cover with a damp towel, and let the dough rise in a warm area until it has doubled in volume.

• Pour the hot water over the tomatoes, and allow them to sit for 30 minutes. Drain, cut into fine julienne, and set aside.

• Punch the dough down, and roll it into a large circle on a floured board. Place the circle on an oiled round pizza pan or baking sheet. Spread the tomatoes, cheese, and herbs to within 1 inch of the edge of the dough, drizzle with the ¼ cup of olive oil, then bake for about 20 minutes, or until the edges of the dough are golden brown.

Wine recommendation: Beaujolais or other fruity red

SOUPS

Creamy Clam Chowder

Four Servings

10 quahogs or 12 cherrystone clams, well scrubbed
1 cup water
½ cup ¼-inch-diced fatback
2 tablespoons butter
1 cup small-diced Spanish onion
1 cup small-diced celery
3 tablespoons flour

1 cup bottled clam juice or fish stock
1 cup large-diced potatoes
1 bay leaf
⅔ cup heavy cream
salt and white pepper as needed
¼ cup chopped fresh parsley

• Place the clams and water in a small saucepan. Cover, and simmer until all the clams have opened. Remove from the fire. Remove the clams from their shells, and mince finely (into approximately ⅛-inch pieces). Set them and their broth aside.

• Render the fatback in a heavy-gauge pot over a medium flame until crispy and dark brown. Remove with a slotted or perforated spoon, and set aside.

• Add the butter to the rendered fat. When melted, add the

onion and celery, and sauté, covered, for 2 or 3 minutes. Add the flour, and cook another minute, stirring continuously.

- Add the clams, reserved broth, bottled clam juice or fish stock, potatoes, and bay leaf. Simmer 15 minutes, stirring frequently.
- Add the cream, and season with salt and white pepper. Simmer another 5 minutes. Serve garnish with the browned cubes of fatback and the chopped parsley.

Wine recommendation: dry Riesling

Philadelphia Pepper Pot Soup

Six Servings

8 ounces tripe	2 tablespoons chicken fat
1 medium Spanish onion, cut into small dice	1 heaping tablespoon flour
1 stalk celery, cut into small dice	2 medium potatoes, peeled and cut into small dice
½ green bell pepper, cut into small dice	2 sprigs fresh thyme
1 medium leek, dark green tops removed, cut into small dice, and well rinsed	2 bay leaves
	1 quart chicken stock
	1 large egg yolk
	1 cup half-and-half or light cream
	salt and pepper as needed

- Cook the tripe in simmering lightly salted water for 2½ hours. Drain, reserving the liquid, and cut into ¼-inch pieces.
- Sauté the onion, celery, green pepper, and leek in the chicken fat in a 1-gallon soup pot for about 5 minutes.
- Blend in the flour thoroughly.
- Add the potato, thyme, bay leaves, tripe, reserved tripe stock, and chicken stock. Stir in thoroughly.
- Simmer for 30 minutes.
- Place the egg yolk and half-and-half in a bowl. Very slowly, ladle hot soup into the bowl, stirring continuously. After approximately half of the soup has been whipped into the yolk-and-cream mixture, return it to the remaining soup. Bring just to a light simmer—do not boil. Season to taste with salt and pepper.

Wine recommendation: dry gewürztraminer

Tripe is the lining of the stomach of a cow, pig, or sheep and has been appreciated in assorted cultures since both Athenaeus and Homer praised it in ancient Greece. Rich in protein and gelatin, it requires long cooking to make it palatable and considerable seasoning to make it tasty. One of the best-known preparations of this dish is Tripe à la mode de Caen, in which the tripe is cooked in an earthenware dish for 10 to 12 hours and flavored with Normandy's apple brandy, calvados.

Escarole is a broad-leafed variety of endive, a member of the daisy family. It is slightly bitter, with a very strong leaf, and stands up well to cooking.

Navy Bean, Escarole, and Garlic Soup

Ten Servings

½ cup dry navy beans, culled, rinsed, and soaked in 3 cups cold water for 12 hours
1 quart water
small ham bone
1 head garlic, cloves separated and peeled
¼ cup water
2 small bay leaves
2 sprigs fresh thyme
6 tablespoons (¾ stick) butter
1 small Spanish onion, cut into small dice

1 small carrot, peeled and cut into small dice
2 stalks celery, cut into small dice
1 small white turnip, peeled and cut into small dice
¼ cup dry white wine
2 quarts chicken stock
½ head escarole, cleaned and torn into ½-inch pieces
salt and pepper as needed

- Preheat an oven to 350° F.
- Drain the beans, then place them in a pot with the ham bone and water. Bring to a boil, and simmer for 1 hour, or until the beans are tender.
- Place the garlic, water, a bay leaf, and 1 sprig of thyme in a small ovenproof pan. Roast for 45 minutes, adding water as needed. Remove from the oven, discarding the bay leaf and thyme, and puree.
- Sauté the diced vegetables in the butter in a soup pot over medium flame, covered, for 5 minutes. Add the white wine, and simmer uncovered for 5 minutes. Add the stock, pureed garlic, second bay leaf and sprig of thyme, beans, and escarole, and simmer for 15 minutes. Season to taste with salt and pepper.

Wine recommendation: dry gewürztraminer

SALADS

Thai Beef Salad

Four Servings

¾ pound medium-rare roasted fillet of beef, cut into julienne
½ cup fish sauce (*nam pla*)
½ cup lime juice
2 tablespoons granulated sugar

3 garlic cloves, minced
1 teaspoon dried red pepper flakes
1 head green leaf lettuce, washed, dried, and torn into bite-size pieces
2 limes, sliced paper-thin

- Combine the julienned beef with all of the other ingredients, except for the lettuce. Mix well, and marinate at least 2 hours.
- Arrange a bed of lettuce on each of 4 individual serving plates. Top with the marinated beef. Garnish with slices of lime.

Spicy Rabbit Salad, with Corn Bread Croutons

Four Servings

FOR THE VINAIGRETTE
½ cup safflower oil
3 tablespoons red wine vinegar

¼ teaspoon dry mustard
pinch salt
pinch pepper

FOR THE SALAD
2 boneless rabbit loins, cleaned and trimmed
3 tablespoons Cajun spice mix (equal parts parsley, sage, thyme, cayenne pepper, paprika, cumin, and black pepper)
2 tablespoons peanut oil

an assortment of dandelion greens, arugula, escarole, and curly endive, enough for 4 servings, cut into bite-size pieces, well washed, and dried
½ cup ¼-inch-square cornbread croutons

TO PREPARE THE VINAIGRETTE
- Puree all of the vinaigrette ingredients together in a blender.

TO PREPARE THE SALAD
- Preheat an oven to 375° F.
- Roll the rabbit loins in the Cajun spice mix.
- Heat the peanut oil in a cast-iron skillet or other ovenproof pan. Brown the rabbit in the oil, then place in the oven for 8 minutes. Remove, and set aside.
- Turn the oven down to 350° F. Place the croutons on a baking sheet, and toast for 15 minutes.
- Toss the greens in the vinaigrette, and arrange on 4 serving plates.
- Slice the rabbit loins very thin, and arrange the slices on top of the greens. Sprinkle with the croutons, and serve.

Spinach Salad, Honey Vinaigrette

Six Servings

FOR THE VINAIGRETTE
1 cup olive oil
⅓ cup red wine vinegar
2 tablespoons water
1 tablespoon honey
½ small Spanish onion,
   roughly chopped

1 teaspoon Dijon mustard
pinch salt
pinch black pepper

FOR THE SALAD
1 small bunch fresh baby spinach leaves, well rinsed and stems trimmed and discarded
1 small head Boston lettuce

2 navel oranges, peeled and cut into individual seedless segments
¼ pound select button mushrooms

TO PREPARE THE VINAIGRETTE
- Puree all of the vinaigrette ingredients in a blender or food processor. Set aside.

TO PREPARE THE SALAD
- Place the lettuce and baby spinach in a bowl, and toss with some of the vinaigrette. Arrange on 4 chilled serving plates. Top with the orange segments and mushrooms, and drizzle a little more vinaigrette on top.

Main Courses

FISH

Grilled Salmon with Creamed Fennel

Four Servings

FOR THE FENNEL

1 whole fennel root,
   trimmed (reserving 3
   stems for the marinade),
   cleaned, and sliced very
   thin

2 tablespoons butter
¾ cup cream
pinch salt
pinch pepper

FOR THE SALMON

1 2-pound fresh salmon
   fillet, skinned
¼ cup melted butter

¼ cup vegetable oil
1 shallot, minced
1 tablespoon Pernod

TO PREPARE THE FENNEL

- Sauté the fennel in the butter for 2 or 3 minutes. Add the cream, salt, and pepper, then simmer until reduced by two-thirds. Set aside.

TO PREPARE THE SALMON

- Slice the salmon at a 45° angle into roughly 8 4-ounce portions.
- Mince the reserved fennel stems, and place in a bowl with the marinade ingredients. Add the salmon.
- Prepare an outdoor grill. Grill the salmon fillets approxi-

Catfish are omnivorous scavengers and bottom feeders. For this reason, they have not been particularly esteemed by gourmands as a source of food. With the recent advent of farm-raised catfish, however, this has changed. Raised under supervised farming conditions, these fish possess a fine-grained, sweet, and delicate flesh with few bones and are an exceptional delicacy.

Catfish are also extremely adaptable. The American bullhead species can survive out of water for several hours; African catfish bury themselves in mud for months to survive rainless periods; still others have internal air sacs that permit them to breathe while traveling from one pond to another.

mately 3 minutes on each side. Serve accompanied by the fennel.

Wine recommendation: dry Riesling

Fried Catfish, Mustard-Pecan Mayonnaise

Four Servings

FOR THE MAYONNAISE

¾ cup mayonnaise
4 tablespoons grainy mustard
½ cup toasted chopped pecans

juice of 1 lemon
salt and pepper as needed

FOR THE CATFISH

4 5-ounce catfish fillets
salt and pepper as needed
½ cup flour
2 large eggs, beaten with 2 tablespoons water

½ cup finely ground cornmeal
¼ cup peanut oil
1 tablespoon unsalted butter

TO PREPARE THE MAYONNAISE

- Blend the first 4 ingredients together, then season to taste with salt and pepper. Refrigerate until ready to serve.

TO PREPARE THE CATFISH

- Season the fish lightly with salt and pepper. Dust with the flour, dip into the egg, then coat with the cornmeal, pressing it onto the fillets. Shake off any excess.
- Heat the oil and butter in a cast-iron skillet over a medium flame. Sauté the fillets until golden brown on both sides. Drain on absorbent paper, then place on appropriate serving plates accompanied by the pecan mayonnaise.

Wine recommendation: rich chardonnay

SHELLFISH

Sea Scallops, Saffron and Pepper Cream

Four Servings

1½ pounds sea scallops
salt, pepper, and flour as
   needed
2 tablespoons olive oil
¼ cup dry white wine

1 large shallot, minced
1 garlic clove, minced
2 pinches saffron
2 cups heavy cream
black pepper as needed

- Pat the scallops dry with a clean towel. Sprinkle them lightly with salt and pepper, then dust them lightly with flour. Sauté in the olive oil over high heat for 1 minute, browning them all over. Remove with a slotted or perforated spoon, and set aside. Wipe out the pan with a clean paper towel.
- Add the wine, shallot, garlic, and saffron to the pan, and simmer until reduced by half. Add the cream, and again simmer until reduced almost by half. Strain.
- Nap 4 warm individual serving plates with sauce, and arrange some of the scallops on the center of each plate. Using a pepper mill, grind a liberal amount of pepper on and around the scallops, and serve.

Wine recommendation: dry chenin blanc

Lobster Elicetche

Four Servings

FOR THE COURT BOUILLON
3 quarts water
1 quart dry white wine
1 cup wine vinegar
3 tablespoons salt
15 black peppercorns,
   crushed

3 bay leaves
2 sprigs fresh thyme
1 stalk celery
1 small Spanish onion,
   peeled and quartered
1 bunch parsley stems

FOR THE LOBSTER

4 1½- to 1¾-pound live
  lobsters
1 large shallot
1 tablespoon butter
2 cups port
1 cup heavy cream

6 tablespoons (¾ stick)
  unsalted butter, cut into
  ½-inch cubes
pinch salt
pinch cayenne pepper

TO PREPARE THE COURT BOUILLON

- Bring all the ingredients to a boil, and simmer for 1 hour. Strain, discard the solids, and return the liquid to the fire.

TO PREPARE THE LOBSTER

- Drop the lobsters into the court bouillon, and simmer for 12 minutes. Remove, and allow to cool.
- Split the tails, crack the claws, and remove all of the meat. Cut it into 1-inch pieces, and set it aside.
- Sauté the shallot in the butter for 3 minutes. Add the port, and reduce by two-thirds. Add the cream, and reduce by half.
- Whip in the butter until it is completely emulsified. Remove from the fire. Season to taste with salt and cayenne pepper.
- Divide the lobster meat among 4 serving bowls. Pour the sauce over it, and serve.

Wine recommendation: dry Riesling

POULTRY

Chicken and Cream, with Biscuits and Corn Relish

Four Servings

FOR THE BISCUITS

2 cups flour
2½ teaspoons baking
  powder
½ teaspoon salt

6 tablespoons (¾ stick)
  unsalted butter, softened
¾ cup milk
1 large egg, beaten

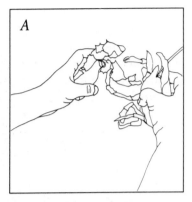

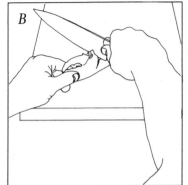

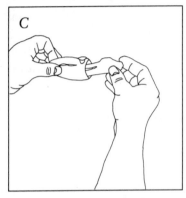

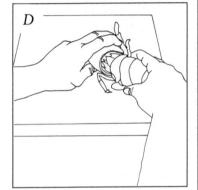

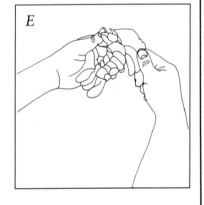

Break the claws from the main body (*A*). Crack the claws using the heel of a knife (*B*). Remove the claw meat (*C*). Tear the tail from the main body (*D*). Carefully tear open the underside of the tail to remove the meat (*E*).

FOR THE RELISH
2 cups cider vinegar
½ cup granulated sugar
1 tablespoon salt
½ teaspoon celery seed
½ teaspoon mustard seed
6 ears fresh corn, kernels removed and cobs discarded
¼ head white cabbage, cut into ½-inch pieces
1 large white onion, diced
1 green bell pepper, cut into ¼-inch squares
1 red bell pepper, cut into ¼-inch squares
½ jalapeño pepper, split, seeded, and sliced very thin

FOR THE CHICKEN

1½ pounds boneless chicken breast, cut into strips

3 tablespoons butter

½ cup sliced mushrooms

½ red bell pepper, cut into ½-inch dice

½ green bell pepper, cut into ½-inch dice

½ jalapeño pepper, seeded and sliced thin

2 cups heavy cream

salt and pepper as needed

TO PREPARE THE BISCUITS

- Preheat an oven to 375° F.
- Combine the flour, baking powder, salt, and butter in a mixing bowl. Rub together between your palms until the mixture resembles coarse meal. Add all but 2 tablespoons of the milk. Gently press the dough into a ball.
- Roll out the dough on a lightly floured surface to a thickness of 1 inch. Cut out 1½- to 2-inch circles, using a cookie cutter (should yield 8 biscuits). Transfer to a lightly buttered baking sheet.
- Combine the 2 remaining tablespoons of milk with the egg, and brush this glaze onto the dough circles. Bake for 15 to 20 minutes, or until golden brown.

TO PREPARE THE RELISH

- Combine the vinegar, sugar, salt, celery seed, and mustard seed in a saucepan. Bring to a boil, and simmer for 5 minutes. Add the vegetables, and simmer another 3 minutes, then refrigerate in a covered container until ready to serve.

TO PREPARE THE CHICKEN

- Sauté the chicken in the butter in a large skillet or sauté pan. Add the mushrooms and peppers, and sauté another 2 minutes. Add the cream to the pan, and simmer until reduced by half. Season to taste with salt and pepper.

TO SERVE

- Split 4 biscuits in half. Place each bottom half on a serving plate, and top with a quarter of the chicken mixture. Place the top half of the biscuit on this, and serve with an additional biscuit and a side of corn relish.

Wine recommendation: light Grenache or rich chardonnay

Brace of Roast Quail, Black Trumpet Mushrooms

Four Servings

8 ounces black trumpet
  mushrooms, cleaned and
  cut into ½-inch pieces
1 large shallot, minced
2 tablespoons butter
pinch salt
pinch pepper
¼ cup brandy or cognac

8 fresh glove-boned quail
vegetable oil as needed
1½ cups chicken stock
3 tablespoons unsalted
  butter, cut into ½-inch
  cubes
salt and pepper as needed

- Preheat an oven to 400° F.
- Sauté the mushrooms and shallot in the butter for about 5 minutes. Add the salt, pepper, and brandy, then simmer until almost completely dry.
- Stuff the quail with the mushroom mixture. Close the opening of each with one or two toothpicks.
- Rub the quail with vegetable oil, and roast for 15 to 20 minutes, or until golden brown. Remove, and set aside, keeping warm.
- Pour the excess oil from the roasting pan. Deglaze with the chicken stock, and simmer until reduced by half.
- Add the butter, stirring continuously until it is completely emulsified. Season to taste with salt and pepper.
- Remove the toothpicks, and serve 2 quail per person, topped with the sauce and accompanied by roast potatoes and a seasonal vegetable.

Wine recommendation: cabernet sauvignon or Pinot Noir

Truffled Breast of Pheasant, with Risotto

Four Servings

FOR THE PHEASANT
4 boneless pheasant breast
  halves, skin on, with the
  first wing joints intact

2 whole fresh truffles
salt and pepper as needed

A member of the chanterelle family, black trumpets are vase- or funnel-shaped mushrooms measuring from ⅜ to 3¼ inches across and 1¼ to 5½ inches tall. Possessing a fruity fragrance and flavor, their flesh is thin and brittle, varying in color from gray to dark brown or black.

Black trumpets can be found throughout North America from July to November, most commonly under oak, beech, and other deciduous trees. WARNING: Many wild mushrooms are extremely poisonous. We recommend gathering them ONLY with an experienced mycologist.

FOR THE SAUCE

4 tablespoons (½ stick) butter

2 shallots, minced

½ cup brandy

1½ cups heavy cream

salt, pepper, and lemon juice as needed

FOR THE RISOTTO

1 medium Spanish onion, minced

2 garlic cloves, minced

2 tablespoons olive oil

2 tablespoons butter

1 bay leaf

2 cups Italian rice

½ teaspoon salt

¼ teaspoon freshly ground white pepper

1 cup assorted wild mushrooms, cut into ¼-inch pieces

5 cups chicken or game stock

FOR SERVING

1 whole fresh black truffle

TO PREPARE THE PHEASANT

- Slice 2 of the truffles very thin. Gently separate the skin from each pheasant breast, leaving it attached along one side. Season the breast meat and skin lightly with salt and pepper, then place a layer of sliced truffles on each breast, underneath the skin. Cover with plastic wrap, and refrigerate overnight.
- Preheat an oven to 350° F.
- Sauté the breasts, skin side down, in an ovenproof skillet or sauté pan until they are light brown. Turn over, then place the pan in the oven, and roast for 10 to 12 minutes. Remove the breasts from the pan, and set aside in a warm place.

TO PREPARE THE SAUCE

- Melt the butter in the ovenproof pan, and sauté the shallots. Deglaze with the brandy, and simmer until almost dry. Add the cream, and simmer until reduced by about half. Strain, and season to taste with salt, pepper, and lemon juice.

TO PREPARE THE RISOTTO

- Sauté the onion and garlic in the oil and butter for 4 or 5 minutes. Add the bay leaf and rice, and cook another few minutes. Add the salt, pepper, mushrooms, and stock. Cover, and cook over a very low flame for 20 to 30 minutes, or until all the liquid has been absorbed.

TO SERVE
- Heat the breasts in the oven for a few minutes, then remove to appropriate serving plates. Place a portion of the risotto next to each serving of pheasant. Top with ¼ cup of the sauce, and grate the truffle over each serving.

Wine recommendation: rich cabernet sauvignon or Pinot Noir

VEAL AND BEEF

Veal Shank Braised in Apple Cider with Lemon Thyme

Four Servings

4 2-inch-thick slices veal shank	2 cups pearl onions
salt, pepper, and flour as needed	16 baby carrots, peeled
¼ cup olive oil	2 cups cherry tomatoes
2 tablespoons butter	¼ cup tomato puree
2 shallots, minced	1 cup apple cider
1 head garlic, cloves peeled	1 cup beef stock
	4 to 6 sprigs fresh lemon thyme

- Preheat an oven to 375° F.
- Season the shanks with salt and pepper, and dust them with flour.
- Heat the oil and butter in a braising pan large enough to hold all the ingredients. Brown the shanks on both sides. Remove, and set aside.
- Sauté the shallots, onion, garlic, and carrots in the braising pan for 5 minutes. Blend in the tomatoes and tomato puree, and cook for 3 minutes. Thoroughly blend in the cider, stock, and lemon thyme. Return the shanks to the pan, bring the sauce to a simmer, cover, and place the pan in the oven. Braise for 1½ hours, turning the shanks every 20 minutes.
- Remove from the oven, and taste the sauce for seasoning.

Serve the shanks with rice pilaf or egg noodles, topped liberally with the sauce and vegetables.

Wine recommendation: rich cabernet sauvignon

Veal Scallops with Walnuts and Smithfield Ham, with Polenta

Four Servings

FOR THE POLENTA

3 cups chicken stock
pinch salt
pinch pepper

⅔ cup yellow cornmeal
6 tablespoons (¾ stick) unsalted butter

FOR THE VEAL

4 4- to 5-ounce veal scallops, pounded very thin
salt, pepper, and flour as needed
4 tablespoons (½ stick) unsalted butter

1 cup thinly sliced mushrooms
½ cup finely julienned Smithfield ham
½ cup chopped walnuts
½ cup dry white wine
2 cups heavy cream

TO PREPARE THE POLENTA

• Bring the chicken stock, salt, and pepper to a boil. Stir in the cornmeal. Reduce the heat to very low, and simmer, stirring constantly, for 20 minutes. Add the butter, and incorporate it thoroughly. Remove from the fire, cover, and set aside.

TO PREPARE THE VEAL

• Season the veal lightly with salt and pepper. Dust lightly with flour. Sauté in the butter over a medium flame for about 1 minute on each side. Remove from the pan, and set aside.
• Add the mushrooms, ham, and walnuts to the pan, and sauté for 3 minutes. Add the wine, and simmer until reduced by half. Add the cream, and simmer until reduced by about one-third. Season to taste with salt and pepper. Return the veal to the sauce, and heat.
• Divide the polenta among 4 serving plates, making a small

well in the center of each serving. Place the veal beside the polenta, and fill the well with some of the sauce.

Wine recommendation: merlot or Pinot Noir

Roast Loin of Veal, Shallot Compote

Eight Servings

FOR THE COMPOTE

4 cups sliced shallots
¼ cup olive oil
5 tablespoons granulated sugar
2 cups dry white wine

¼ cup cider vinegar
pinch saffron
pinch salt
pinch pepper

FOR THE VEAL

1 3-pound (approximate weight) veal strip loin, trimmed of all fat and silver skin

2 garlic cloves, minced
salt and pepper as needed
¼ cup olive oil

TO PREPARE THE COMPOTE

- Sauté the shallots in the olive oil over a medium flame, covered, for 10 minutes, stirring occasionally. Do not allow to brown.
- Add the sugar, and cook until dissolved. Add the remaining ingredients, and simmer until reduced by three-quarters. Remove from the fire, and set aside until ready to serve.

TO PREPARE THE VEAL

- Preheat an oven to 350° F.
- Rub the veal loin with the minced garlic. Season with salt and pepper.
- Brown the loin on all sides in the olive oil. Place in the oven, and roast for 12 to 15 minutes. Remove from the oven, and allow to rest 10 minutes. Slice thin, and serve with the warm shallot compote.

Wine recommendation: soft merlot or cabernet sauvignon

Mincing garlic can be a tedious chore, and it leaves the scent of garlic on the hands, as well as on the knife and board. We recommend using a good garlic press, which purees the garlic cloves. If you are a true garlic aficionado, one or more heads can be peeled, then pureed in a food processor with a little olive oil. Tightly covered and refrigerated, garlic prepared this way will keep its potency for up to 2 weeks.

Shallot is a mild member of the onion family, possessing a slight flavor of garlic. Considered by some to be more easily digested than its relatives, it is essential to the production of many finished sauces. Its name comes from Askalon, a Western Mediterranean trading center where it was a popular vegetable.

Veal Scallops, South Philadelphia Style

Four Servings

8 3-ounce veal scallops,
   pounded very thin
salt, pepper, and flour as
   needed
¼ cup olive oil
2 cups sliced mushrooms

½ cup Madeira
¾ cup demi-glace
4 tablespoons (½ stick)
   unsalted butter, cut into
   ½-inch cubes

- Season the veal scallops lightly with salt and pepper, and dust them lightly with flour.
- Heat the olive oil in a sauté pan, and sauté the scallops lightly on both sides. Remove, and set aside.
- Add the mushrooms, and sauté until they are light brown. Add the Madeira, and simmer until reduced by half. Add the demi-glace, and simmer until the desired consistency is reached.
- Stir in the butter until it is completely emulsified. Return the veal scallops to the pan, heat, and serve on a bed of buttered egg noodles.

Wine recommendation: light Pinot Noir

Tenderloin of Beef, Onion Sauce

Four Servings

FOR THE SAUCE
2 cups baby onions
   (*cipolline*), peeled and
   sliced into thin circles
4 tablespoons (½ stick)
   unsalted butter

1 tablespoon Dijon mustard
2 tablespoons dry red wine
1 cup demi-glace
salt and pepper as needed

FOR THE BEEF
8 4-ounce beef tenderloin
   steaks, trimmed of all fat
   and sinew
Dijon mustard and cracked
   black peppercorns as
   needed

¼ cup olive oil

TO PREPARE THE SAUCE
- Sauté the onions in the butter over a medium flame, stirring frequently, for about 20 minutes, or until they are golden brown.
- Pour off any excess butter. Mix the mustard with the wine, and add to the onions. Add the demi-glace. Simmer 5 minutes or so, continuously skimming impurities from the top. Adjust seasoning, and set aside.

TO PREPARE THE BEEF
- Lightly coat the steaks with mustard and peppercorns. Heat the olive oil over a medium flame. Cook the steaks on both sides to desired degree of doneness. Serve 2 steaks per person, topped with the onion sauce.

Wine recommendation: zinfandel or cabernet sauvignon

Final Courses

COLD DESSERTS

In the absence of a small loaf pan, any metal mold will suffice, even a small stainless steel bowl. Just keep in mind what shape you wish the terrine to have as you are choosing a container.

Bittersweet Chocolate Terrine, Ginger Cream

Four Servings

FOR THE TERRINE

4 ounces semisweet chocolate, broken into small pieces

4 tablespoons (½ stick) unsalted butter

2 eggs, separated

1 tablespoon Grand Marnier

butter as needed

FOR THE CREAM

2 large egg yolks

3 tablespoons granulated sugar

2 teaspoons grated fresh ginger root

1 cup milk

FOR SERVING

powdered sugar

8 fresh mint leaves

TO PREPARE THE TERRINE

- Place the chocolate and butter in the top half of a double boiler, and melt over barely simmering water, stirring occasionally.
- Remove from the fire, and allow to cool.
- Thoroughly blend in the egg yolks and the Grand Marnier.
- In a separate bowl, beat the egg whites to stiff peaks, then carefully fold them into the chocolate mixture.
- Butter a small loaf pan. Place a piece of wax or parchment paper, cut to fit the inside bottom, into the pan, and spread it with a little butter.

Use extra small

- Pour the chocolate mixture into the pan, smooth the top with a rubber spatula, and refrigerate for at least 4 hours.

TO PREPARE THE CREAM
- In a small mixing bowl, whip together the yolks, the sugar, and the ginger until the mixture is thick and light lemon colored.
- Heat the milk until it just begins to simmer. Ladle the hot milk very slowly into the whipped eggs, stirring continuously. Return this mixture to the pan, and heat over a medium flame, stirring continuously, until the mixture is slightly thickened and smooth and coats the back of the spoon. Chill for 2 hours.

TO SERVE
- When ready to serve, dip the mousse pan in very hot water for 5 seconds or so. Pat it dry, then invert it onto a plate. For each serving, ladle about ¼ cup of the sauce onto a serving plate. Slice the terrine, place a slice on top of the sauce on each plate, and garnish with powdered sugar and 2 mint leaves.

CAKES AND BREADS

Buttermilk Baby Cakes, Cranberry-Raspberry Sauce

Twelve Servings

FOR THE SAUCE
2 cups whole fresh (or fresh-frozen) cranberries
¾ cup honey
¼ cup orange juice

1 pint dry-pack frozen raspberries
¼ cup kirsch, or cherry brandy

FOR THE CAKES
2 cups cake flour
1½ cups granulated sugar
⅛ teaspoon kosher salt
2 teaspoons baking soda
½ cup vegetable oil

¾ cup buttermilk
1 teaspoon vanilla
6 large egg whites
¼ teaspoon cream of tartar

TO PREPARE THE SAUCE

- Combine the cranberries, honey, and orange juice in a small saucepan. Bring to a boil, and simmer 7 or 8 minutes. Add the raspberries, and simmer another 5 minutes. Remove from the fire.
- Puree the fruit mixture with the kirsch in a blender or food processor. Strain through a fine sieve. Set aside until ready to serve.

TO PREPARE THE CAKES

- Preheat an oven to 350° F. Butter and lightly flour 12 4-inch baking pans.
- Combine the flour, half of the sugar, the salt, baking soda, oil, buttermilk, and vanilla in a mixing bowl. Beat with a hand electric mixer into a smooth batter.
- In another bowl, beat the egg whites, adding the cream of tartar and remaining sugar slowly, until they form stiff peaks. Fold gently into the batter in two batches.
- Pour the batter into the prepared baking pans. Bake for 35 minutes. Remove from the oven, allow to cool 10 minutes, then remove from the pans. Serve warm, with the warm sauce.

PIES

Pear Almond Tart

Eight to Ten Servings

FOR THE CRUST

7½ ounces blanched almonds
½ cup granulated sugar
1 cup flour
¼ teaspoon salt

9 tablespoons (1 stick plus 1 tablespoon) unsalted butter
2 large egg yolks
¼ cup white bread crumbs

FOR THE FILLING

3 large eggs
3/4 cup granulated sugar
1 teaspoon vanilla extract

1/4 cup flour
1/2 cup melted unsalted
   butter

FOR ASSEMBLY

2 or 3 pears, peeled, cored,
  and sliced

4 ounces sliced blanched
  almonds

TO PREPARE THE CRUST

- Grind the almonds in a food processor with half of the sugar. Add the remaining dry ingredients, and process until blended.
- Transfer to a mixing bowl. Thoroughly blend in the butter, a little at a time, and then the egg yolks.
- Sprinkle the breadcrumbs on the inside bottom of a lightly buttered 8- or 9-inch quiche, tart, or pie pan. Press the dough into the pan.

TO PREPARE THE FILLING

- Beat the eggs, sugar, and vanilla together until the sugar is dissolved. Blend in the flour, then stir in the melted butter.

TO ASSEMBLE THE TART

- Preheat an oven to 350° F.
- Arrange the pear slices on the crust. Pour the filling over them, sprinkle with the almonds, and bake for 30 to 45 minutes, or until the almonds are golden brown. Cool and serve.

There exist several thousand varieties of pears and apples throughout the world, most of these developed in the eighteenth and nineteenth centuries. Only about a hundred varieties of each are cultivated commercially.

That apples are more popular than pears may have to do with the fact that pears are far more delicate and more prone to damage in adverse weather conditions. Pears are also one of the few fruits that do not mature well if allowed to ripen on the tree. An unripe pear will ripen nicely, however, increasing in sugar and moisture content, when left standing at room temperature for a few days.

COOKIES

The macadamia nut actually is native to the northeastern coast of Australia. It comes from a small evergreen tree that was named in 1858 for John Macadam, a Scottish-born chemist. The outer shell of the nut is extremely tough, requiring several hundred pounds of pressure to crack. Introduced to Hawaii in the 1890s, it became commercially important in the 1930s.

White Chocolate Chunk–Macadamia Nut Cookies

Two Dozen Cookies

8 tablespoons (1 stick) unsalted butter
½ cup light brown sugar
¼ cup granulated sugar
2 large eggs
2 teaspoons vanilla extract
1 cup plus 2 tablespoons flour
½ teaspoon baking soda
¼ teaspoon salt
7 ounces white chocolate, coarsely chopped
1 cup macadamia nuts, coarsely chopped

- Preheat an oven to 300° F.
- Beat the butter and sugars in a mixing bowl until smooth and creamy. Thoroughly blend in the egg and vanilla.
- Blend in the dry ingredients, being careful not to overmix. Stir in the chocolate and nuts.
- Spoon the batter by heaping tablespoonfuls, approximately 2 inches apart, onto a baking sheet, and bake 10 to 12 minutes, or until the cookies are golden brown.

Grown in the USA

The food service industry has grown and changed dramatically in recent years, and it continues to grow and change, in response to an enlightened public. The food we grew up on has given way to a higher standard of excellence. Fresh, minimally cooked vegetables have replaced frozen and overcooked ones; fresh herbs have upstaged the dried, packaged variety; fine domestic camembert, brie, and blue cheese have challenged processed, individually wrapped mock-cheese slices; sparkling chardonnays and vintage Pinot Noirs have replaced cold duck and screw-top jug wines; wines and juices patiently fermented in oak barrels have produced the first generation of quality American vinegars. Clearly, our collective palate has evolved, and an extraordinary industry of specialty food producers has evolved along with it. This community of enterprising and innovative individuals has played a significant role in today's culinary renaissance.

It is the end of February 1989, and I am traveling south from Portland, on my way to a meeting with a grower in Brownsville, Oregon, in the eastern Willamette Valley. With me are George Poston, chef de cuisine of Atwater's Restaurant in Portland, and Billy Della Ventura, my literary assistant and a fine chef in his own right.

When we arrive, we find George H. Weppler in the greenhouse packing several plastic-lined boxes with a variety of young lettuces and herbs. We are surrounded by fresh herbs and row upon row of dozens of varieties of barely sprouted lettuces. It is a delicious sight.

The moderate climate in the Willamette Valley supports all kinds of agriculture. Some crops are grown year-round; others thrive seasonally. In all, Weppler Farms produces over two hundred varieties of produce, which are harvested, washed,

chilled, and shipped to customers on the same day that orders arrive to ensure top quality and maximum shelf life.

"It's been a tough year," George says. "You guys heard about the freeze, didn't you?" We nod yes. "This past winter, we had the coldest temperature ever recorded in this part of the state—zero degrees—with temperatures as cold as −40° F in other parts of the state. Most of my lettuces were destroyed." He takes us outside, showing us the damage. "It's okay, though. This soil is very rich. The Calapooya River, not far from here now, once flowed over this land. As a result, it is very fertile. I should have another crop of baby romaine, some mache, and a couple of varieties of purple basil in a month or two."

"This farm life is healthy and rewarding. With Mother Nature on your side, plenty of hard work, and what I call pioneer ingenuity, you can grow beautiful produce. For instance, this area is full of wildlife, including deer. They love to stop here for a snack. I needed to find a way to discourage this, without disrupting their lifestyle—after all, they were here long before any of us. So I thought about it for a while and came up with the idea of stringing nylon fishing line around the crops, about four feet off the ground. When the deer come strolling in looking for a quick bite, they run into the line. They can't see it, so, to them, it feels like some kind of invisible force field. It's enough to keep them at bay. They still come around, and we're on good terms, but they leave my vegetables alone."

George's well-muscled physique belies his background. Fourteen years ago, he and his wife and children lived in Los Angeles, where George was a successful biology researcher working for a major bottled water company. "We had it all. But I just couldn't keep up with that urban rat race. So we moved up to this farm. I like to grow things—in fact, I have been growing plants for nearly forty years. My two degrees, one in biology, and one in business administration, both help with what I'm doing now. I ship my vegetables and herbs all over the country—Boston, Houston, Miami, Chicago, St. Louis, Reno, Anchorage, and of course, here in Oregon. It's challenging work, but very satisfying."

Inside the main house, I notice a computer. "Yes, I use the computer for accounting and to assist in crop rotation. It's a tremendous asset. And my children use it for their schoolwork. We even have a color TV. I guess you can't escape all of it."

George's vegetables are magnificent. Thirty different varieties of lettuce in shades of red, purple, bronze, and green; broadleaf Batavian endive, escarole, and frizzy leaf chicory; spinach varieties—Melody, Indian Summer, Tyee, and American; mache, better known as lamb's lettuce; Purple Pearl and Walla Walla sweet onions; baby leeks, tomatoes, and bok choy, all as fresh and vital as the prized *printanières* celebrated during the spring in Europe; ten different varieties of squash, with or without flowers and in any size desired; and eight different varieties of string beans; and, of course, edible flowers—chrysanthemum, arugula, nasturtium, squash, tatsoi, and calendula. At one point, Billy turns to me and says, "Man, what a great life. I wonder what would happen if we never went back?" It is a seductive thought.

From George Weppler's farm, George Poston headed back to his culinary duties, while Billy and I visited winegrowers, mushroom cultivators, cheese manufacturers, beer breweries, and distilleries. We met with Arly Smith, a jack-of-many-trades who has refined a technique for cultivating shiitake and oyster mushrooms. I had always thought that the cultivation of wild mushroom varieties was a new science; Arly informed us that it was not: wild mushrooms have been cultivated in the Orient for hundreds of years; the United States was just slow to catch on. Arly's method is to drill holes in oak logs, fill them with shiitake sawdust, and then stack the logs carefully in a temperature- and humidity-controlled storehouse. In nine months, the mushrooms sprout, maturing in six to twelve days.

We visited Stephen R. McCarthy, formerly a practicing attorney, now proprietor of Clear Creek Distillery, located right in Portland. He has spent eleven years refining his method of distilling Bartlett pears into an *eau de vie,* a crystal-clear, distilled essence of pears. We toured his production area, where I accepted an invitation to climb to the top of one of the immense fermenting tanks to breathe in the spirited aroma of the Bartlett pear mash. Eventually, we tasted his creation. It was like nothing we had ever tried. Dry fruit brandies, like the German kirschwasser used in pastry work and the Alsatian marcs, tend to be harsh, with the presence of the fruit found only detectable in the bouquet. McCarthy's Bartlett Pear Brandy possessed an intense bouquet that was matched by its mellow flavor. We also sampled some apple brandy that McCarthy has been perfecting for three years and was due for release in late 1989. Again, we found the flavor, bouquet, and consistency to be extraordinarily rich and lush.

At Adelsheim Vineyards, proprietor and winemaker Da-

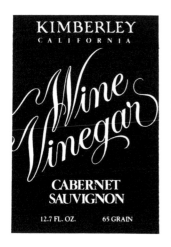

vid B. Adelsheim handed us a dozen or so wine labels, all illustrated with paintings or sketches by his wife, Virginia. I remarked that, often in this country, a specially commissioned artistic label signals an inferior, or at least over-priced, wine. This was not the case here. The Pinot Noirs, chardonnays, merlots, among others, were all remarkable. The extraordinary label art was an accurate tribute to the exceptional wine inside.

Jerry Coates, a retired Blitz-Weinhard Brewery worker, was our host for a specially arranged tour of that establishment. I was familiar with Henry Weinhard's Private Reserve, a beer that has been marketed nationally since 1976, and had presumed that this was the first product of a new brewery. I was surprised to learn that Henry Weinhard had begun the brewery as a young German immigrant in 1860.

Our last stop in Oregon was at the Department of Agriculture, where I was astonished to learn of the extraordinary wealth of food products produced in the state. According to Oregon agricultural statistics, while the number of farms in the United States has diminished by more than 25 percent since 1971, the number of farms in Oregon has increased by nearly 7.5 percent during the same period.

From Oregon, we headed south to San Francisco for a visit to Kimberly Vinegar Works, housed in a weatherworn erstwhile canteen on the grounds of what was once a naval shipyard. We were greeted by Larry and Ruth Robinson and the heady aroma of wine and fermenting yeast. Since 1980, the Robinsons have been using sherry and chardonnay and cabernet wines to create a line of vinegars. Larry Robinson is still a full-time mathematics teacher at a secondary school in San Francisco. Ruth, a former employee of Trans World Airlines, now devotes all of her time to the vinegar production. The company is named after their fourteen year-old daughter.

Vinegar is an indispensable ingredient in many foods—mayonnaise, relishes, pickles, condiments, and candy. It is also found in many household cleaning and health applications. Commercially produced vinegars are the result of a chemical and distilling process that requires three days to complete. The Robinsons employ the Orléans method, a fermentation technique developed in Orléans, France, nearly five hundred years ago. First a liquid starter, a "mother," is introduced into a varietal wine—the proportion is one part starter to seven parts wine—then allowed to ferment in handcrafted oak barrels for five to six months. The Robinsons purchase the barrels from winemakers in both Wisconsin and the Bordeaux region of France after they have been used for several years.

The bacteria in the starter consumes the alcohol in the wine, transforming it into acetic acid and carbon dioxide. Holes drilled in the ends of the barrels allow the gas to vent. After six months, the wine vinegar, then containing 10 percent acetic acid, is carefully filtered and transferred to holding tanks, where impurities are allowed to settle. It is then strained, diluted to 6.5 percent acidity, and bottled. The resulting vinegars, some of which are flavored with garlic or fruit essences, are nothing like commercially produced brews—their bouquets are far more potent and their flavors lively and intense.

Our next stop was Santa Rosa, where we met with Laura Chenel. Years ago, I had been impressed by stories of an enterprising young woman in California who was making a chèvre. I looked forward to meeting her in person.

In the late seventies, Ms. Chenel wanted to learn how to make goat's milk cheese. Unable to do so here, she went to France, where she worked on four different family-run goat cheese farms. There, she learned the generations-old techniques of cheese making and made the decision to apply them back in California.

In France, there is a belief that, if one employs too much high technology, if one is too clean, one cannot produce a flavorful cheese. The state of California, however, has extremely tough sanitation laws governing the manufacture of dairy products. Ms. Chenel has had to adapt the methods she learned in Europe to meet American requirements. "That we employ a more evolved technology here, which protects the consumer, has little to do with what the final product will taste like. The same laws that protect the consumer also protect the manufacturer. But it is the character of the milk, the type of cheese culture, and how the cheese is aged, that determine its final characteristics."

That goat's milk cheese is considerably easier to digest than other cheeses is only one of its virtues. It also boasts only 82 calories per one-ounce serving and contains significant amounts of protein, carbohydrates, vitamins, and minerals. All of Laura Chenel's cheeses are handcrafted, and all are distinctive and flavorful—from fresh, mild varieties coated with different herbs and spices to aged rounds, logs, pyramids, and small cylinders, from slightly aged "buttons" marinated in California olive oil and herbs to the twelve-month-aged "tome."

A little farther up the road, in the town of Sonoma, we visited Ignazio Vella, chief executive officer of the Vella Cheese

Company. Begun in 1931 by his father, Thomas Vella, the Vella Cheese Company is the only company in the United States making a dry variety of Monterey Jack, a cheese created in the mid-nineteenth century by David Jack, a Scottish emigrant residing in Monterey, California. The dry variety has an intriguing story behind it.

Early in the twentieth century in northern California, fresh milk was very much a seasonal product, with availability peaking during the spring. Consequently, cheese manufacturers scheduled their production for that season, usually selling out their fresh cheeses very quickly. Many recent immigrants, however, preferred cheese from the old country, no matter how high the quality of the locally produced varieties. Thus, even though fresh cheese was popular during the spring, hard grating cheeses were imported. World War I changed all of this.

In the spring of 1915, a San Francisco cheese wholesaler, D. F. DeBernardi, made his usual contracts for fresh Monterey Jack cheese to sell fresh until the Romano and Parmesan cheese arrived from Italy. But when Italy entered the war on the side of the Allies, its exportation of hard cheeses came to a halt. To compensate, DeBernardi increased his order for fresh cheese, hand-salting the rounds already in stock to increase their shelf life.

When the hand-salted cheese began to dry out, it developed a sweet, nutty flavor, not unlike medium-cured Parmesan. Realizing that he had stumbled upon a potential substitute for the imported hard grating cheeses, DeBernardi coated the drying cheeses with oil, pepper, and lampblack, the traditional preserving method used in Parma. Throughout the war years, his hard cheese graced many a table, establishing itself as a fine alternative to imported cheese. After the war, other cheese manufacturers and distributors began offering similar dried Jacks; soon, sixty different plants were competing in the market. In the mid-thirties, however, the Depression and a flood of cheap foreign grating cheeses, especially those from South America, put all but two out of business.

To this day, dry Jack is still a hand-crafted, labor-intensive cheese, the production of which defies mechanization. It is formed in muslin sacks, brined, coated with a blend of oil, pepper, and cocoa powder, and finally aged for six to ten months.

From California, we headed out to Chicago and a visit with Carolyn Collins, proprietor of Carolyn Collins Caviar. The gregarious and enthusiastic Ms. Collins, a long-time caviar aficionado, was inspired to begin production of a domestic caviar while fishing on Lake Michigan, when she realized that the roe from the many varieties of fish caught in the lake was being discarded.

Traditionally prepared caviar is made from fresh roe, then cold-stored for year-round sale. Ms. Collins uses a different method, storing the uncured salmon, trout, and sturgeon, then making the caviar to order weekly. She began by selling samples of her product to upscale restaurants around her hometown of Crystal Lake and started full-scale production in 1984. Her company has doubled production every year since then, and, while her annual yield of 16,000 pounds is small compared to the international competition, the "queen of caviar" has earned a national reputation for her products, with praise coming from both professional and amateur cooks and chefs. In addition to trout, salmon, sturgeon, whitefish, and bowfin caviar varieties, she has also innovated Caviar Peppar, a golden whitefish caviar flavored with jalapeño and Absolut Peppar Vodka. "I want to see caviar as popular in the kitchen as tins of sardines." She may get her wish—her caviar is not only a delight to the palate, it is lower in salt and considerably less expensive than the imported variety.

Our next stop was something of an anomaly in the rural flatlands of northern Illinois: housed in a white, windowless building on a country road in DeKalb is a state-of-the-art hydroponic farm, PhytoFarms of America, Inc. Scientist-inventor Noel Davis had developed the system for General Mills in the mid-seventies, but, when that company realized that the rising cost of electricity would forestall a quick return on its investment, it lost interest in the project. Davis bought the technology back from General Mills in 1983, and, even with an annual electric bill of a half million dollars, he has begun to operate at a profit.

Several innovative practices have allowed Davis to remain as one of the few survivors in hydroponic farming. One is to cover each of more than one thousand thousand-watt lamps with a glass casing. Water is pumped through these casings, transferring the heat from each lamp to the factory's heating system. Enough heat is drawn from the lamps in this manner to maintain the temperature of the factory interior during the cold winter months.

"Basically, we transform a lot of electricity, some seeds, and a little water into fresh food," says Davis. Measuring 200-by-250 feet—the area of approximately one acre of land—PhytoFarms produces fifteen thousand pounds of herbs and salad greens each week, each pound requiring five pounds of water infused with nitrogen, phosphorus, potassium, iron, calcium, and other essential nutrients. It would take one hundred acres of arable land to produce the same quantity of food, and ten times the amount of water. Fifty thousand seeds germinate at PhytoFarms each day. Its fifty-five employees plant, nurture, and harvest full heads of Bibb, green leaf, and Boston lettuce in 26 days (compared with 42 to 60 days for outdoor farming). Spinach and herbs require 22 to 28 days.

Every year, the United States loses more than one thousand square miles of farmland to urban sprawl and road construction; more than a quarter of a million babies are born every day. Hydroponic farming is clearly one way to address some of the world's food problems. Several Japanese companies currently are exploring building hydroponic farms. Norway and Sweden, with their abundant hydroelectric power, are also interested. PhytoFarms is working with the University of Wisconsin to conduct a study for NASA on the possibility of growing hydroponic crops on the moon. As Noel Davis puts it, "The world is finally catching up with me."

Traveling east once again, Billy and I stop in Philadelphia to visit the Reading Terminal Market. The origins of this institution can be traced back to the farmers, hunters, and fishermen who set up the first markets in Philadelphia in 1683, one year after William Penn dubbed the triangle of land between the Schuylkill and Delaware Rivers Philadelphia. The first recorded market was established in the vicinity of Front and High streets, where butchers had movable stalls. (High Street is now appropriately called Market Street.) The number of markets grew rapidly as the population of the city increased.

In the middle of the last century, the proliferation of open markets in the metropolitan area was looked upon as a nuisance and a health hazard. Pressure from the streetcar industry, which wanted to locate tracks on Market Street, prompted legislation in 1859 that forced the markets to move inside. Two market houses were built on the northeast corner of Twelfth and Market Streets—the Farmer's Market and the Franklin Market. These were the forebears of today's Reading Terminal Market.

In 1889, the Philadelphia and Reading Railway coveted these market properties as the location for their new headquarters and transportation terminus. Since the two existing markets had proven their value to the city, it was decided to incorporate them into the railroad's plans. A lofty train shed was built above the farmer's stalls, providing easy access to goods coming from outlying farms and a convenient means to send orders out to customers on suburban lines. When the Reading Market Terminal first opened in 1893, it was billed as one of the great markets of the world, the equal of the markets of Paris, Budapest, and Stockholm. It boasted a state-of-the-art underground refrigeration system and a handsome Italian exterior.

But the fortunes of the market did not always match its grand beginnings. The Reading Railroad declined in the years following the Second World War, and officially went out of operation in 1971. By 1980, only twenty-seven merchants remained in operation. In 1981, the Reading Company, the firm that now owns and operates the Terminal Market, decided that revival of the market, given its location in the center of a major urban metropolis and its historical significance, would benefit all parties concerned—economically as well as culturally—and hired David K. O'Neil to manage the market. Mr. O'Neil actively sought to broaden the ethnic representation inside the terminal, to reflect the city's present cultural mix. He also persuaded Amish farmers to open stalls for the first time in the market's history. And now, alongside the Amish, Mennonite, German, and Italian merchants operate Latin, Asian, and Middle Eastern entrepreneurs dealing in wholesale fish and produce, as well as short-order savories. Covering an area of two acres, the market houses roughly eighty different purveyors, accommodates more than fifteen thousand shoppers daily, and has gross annual sales in excess of twenty million dollars. Many of the current merchants are third- and fourth-generation tenants whose great-grandfathers began businesses when the market first opened.

From Philadelphia, we drove north to the Lyon's Brewery in Wilkes-Barre, where Jaime Jurado, the young brewmaster, is charged with the task of brewing more than a dozen different beers. I was familiar with one variety, Nathan Hale Golden Lager, which is based on a recipe tracked down by John Foley, president of The Connecticut Brewing Company. I wanted to meet the man responsible for reinstating this unique beverage in the national beer repertory, so we went to Elmwood, Connecticut, where Foley operates the offices of his brewing business.

Foley describes his approach to brewing as "a mission, a

crusade, to produce a great upscale American beer. I wanted an American beer, so I searched for one—in the archives of the Old State House in Hartford. It took some doing, but I found the oldest recorded beer recipe in the history of the Nutmeg State.

"Imported beer is great when it is consumed in the country in which it is brewed. But it reaches our shores months after it has been brewed, and time and travel are the two worst enemies of beer. We are rather proud to say that Nathan Hale Golden Lager is a fresh beer, one of a handful of beers that have passed the German Purity Law of 1516." This sixteenth-century German statute stipulates that beer can only be produced with four traditional ingredients: malt, hops, yeast, and water. The large national breweries use fillers like rice, corn, and other cereals to keep their production costs down. Not the brewers of Nathan Hale.

Beer has played a significant role in our country's history since the Pilgrims landed at Plymouth Rock (according to legend, because they had run out of beer). By 1873, more than four thousand independent breweries were operating in the United States, many of them taverns run by the British, Irish, German, and Dutch immigrants who had brewed house beers in their taverns and pubs back home. Prohibition put a stop to all this in 1920, and, when it was repealed in 1933, only about seven hundred and fifty breweries reopened. Then, after World War II, a handful of major brewing companies, spurred by technological advances in bottling, transportation, refrigeration, and advertising, merged into conglomerates, devouring most of the remaining small competitors. By 1980, there were only forty breweries in the country.

Foley's interest in brewing began in 1984, with a senior thesis on the future of brewing that he wrote while a student at the University of Notre Dame in Indiana. Graduating with a BBA in management, he pursued his interest, serving an apprenticeship to one of the most respected master brewers in the country. He is just one of dozens of young entrepreneurs behind the new movement in the beer industry that started in 1981. This renaissance in beer appreciation began with the establishment of forty-three new domestic "microbreweries." By 1987, there were eighty-seven new independent breweries in the United States. Foley likens this resurgence of interest in beer to the wine appreciation trend of the seventies, with chablis and chardonnay drinkers now switching to bocks, ales, porters, and stouts. In 1982, the first annual Great American Beer Festival featured forty different beers from twenty-two breweries and attracted seven hundred attendees. In 1988, ninety breweries showcased one hundred and fifty different brews for an audience of more than five thousand.

DAVID PAUL LAROUSSE

APPENDIX
OF SPECIALTY PURVEYORS

The following is a very partial list of some growers, packagers, and producers of food products unique to the United States. Many of them will supply their products by mail; some offer guided tours of their establishments; all furnish some of the finest food items available in this country.

Produce and Wild Mushrooms

CALIFORNIA

PARADISE FARMS, P.O. Box 436, Summerland, CA 93067.
  Send for information on edible flowers.

The following are some of the most established farmers' markets in Northern California. A free *Farmer-to-Consumer Directory* can be obtained by writing to the State of California Department of Food and Agriculture Direct Marketing Program, 1220 N Street, A-287, P.O. Box 942871, Sacramento, CA 94271-0001.

BERKELEY MARKET, Derby Street, between Milvia Street and Martin Luther King Way, Tuesdays, from 2:00 to 7:00 P.M., year-round.

DAVIS MARKET, 4th and C Streets, Wednesdays, from 3:00 to 6:00 P.M., and Saturdays, from 8:00 A.M. to 12:00 P.M., year-round.

FRESNO MARKET, Vineyard Shopping Center, Shaw and Blackstone Avenues, Tuesdays, Thursdays, and Saturdays, from 8:00 A.M. to 12:00 P.M., year-round.

MARIN COUNTY MARKET, Civic Center Fairgrounds, San Rafael, Sundays, from 9:00 A.M. to 2:00 P.M., May through November; Thursdays, from 8:00 A.M. to 1:00 P.M., year-round.

NAPA VALLEY MARKET, Dansk Square, St. Helena, Fridays, from 7:30 A.M. to 12:00 P.M., May through November.

PALO ALTO MARKET, Gilman Street behind the downtown post office, Saturdays, from 9:00 A.M. to 1:00 P.M., June through November.

PLEASANT HILL MARKET, Hope Center parking lot, Hillcrest Center, Saturdays, from 8:00 A.M. to 1:00 P.M., May through November.

REDWOOD CITY MARKET, parking lot on Winslow, south of Broadway, Saturdays, from 8:00 A.M. to 12:00 P.M., June through October.

SACRAMENTO CENTRAL MARKET, under Highway 80 at 8th and W Streets, Sundays, from 8:00 A.M. to 12:00 P.M., year-round.

SAN FRANCISCO ALEMANY MARKET, Tuesdays through Fridays, from 8:30 A.M. to 5:00 P.M., and Saturdays, from 6:00 A.M. to 6:00 P.M., year-round.

SAN FRANCISCO HEART OF THE CITY MARKET, United Nations Plaza, Sundays, Wednesdays, and Fridays, from 8:00 A.M. to 5:00 P.M., year-round.

SANTA ROSA MARKET, Veterans Memorial Building, Wednesdays, from 9:00 A.M. to 12:00 P.M., May through December; Saturdays, from 9:00 A.M. to 12:00 P.M., year-round.

STOCKTON MARKET, downtown under the Crosstown Freeway, Saturdays, from 7:00 A.M. to 12:00 P.M., year-round.

VALLEJO MARKET, downtown on Georgia Street near Santa Clara Street, Saturdays, from 9:00 A.M. to 1:00 P.M., year-round.

WALNUT CREEK MARKET, Walnut Creek Library parking lot, Broadway and Lincoln Streets, Sundays, from 9:00 A.M. to 1:00 P.M., May through November.

ILLINOIS

PHYTOFARMS OF AMERICA, INC., 155 Harvest Drive, DeKalb, IL 60115, telephone (800) 962-7890, Sandy Willrett, sales manager.

OREGON

The following list was supplied by the Oregon Department of Agriculture. For additional information, write them at 121 S.W. Salmon Street, Suite 240, Portland, OR 97204-2987, or telephone (503) 229-6734.

BEAVERTON FARMER'S MARKET, P.O. Box 1425, Beaverton, OR 97075, telephone (503) 643-7910 or 291-2361, Theresa La Hahie, contact.

BLUE MOUNTAIN PRODUCERS CO-OP, 1207 M Avenue, La Grande, OR 97850, telephone (503) 963-8049, Jenny Nicholson, contact.

GRANT'S PASS GROWER'S MARKET, P.O. Box 573, Grant's Pass, OR 97526, telephone (503) 476-5375 or 476-5773, Marty Fate, contact.

GRESHAM FARMER'S MARKET, P.O. Box 1134, Gresham, OR 97030, telephone (503) 665-3214, Lisa Barton-Mullins, contact.

HERMISTON FARMER'S MARKET, Rt. 3, Box 3695, Hermiston, OR 97838, telephone (503) 567-5444, Maurice McDaniel, contact.

HILLSBORO FARMER'S MARKET, 874 N.E. Birchwood Drive, Hillsboro, OR 97124, telephone (503) 648-9755, Merrill Ludlam, contact.

LANE COUNTY FARMER'S MARKET, E. 8th and Oak Streets, Eugene, OR 97401, telephone (503) 344-1799, John Graham, contact.

LINCOLN COUNTY SMALL FARMER'S MARKET, Lincoln County Fairgrounds,

Newport, OR 97365, telephone (503) 528-3050, June Reynolds, contact, 9170 Alsea Highway, Tidewater, OR 97390.

McMinnville Farmer's Market, 23900 S.W. Loganberry Lane, Sheridan, OR 97378, telephone (503) 843-4018, Tony Carson, contact.

Medford Farmer's Market, P.O. Box 1432, Jacksonville, OR 97530, telephone (503) 899-8081, Will Hislebeard, contact.

Mid-Willamette Growers Association, 815 N. 9th, Albany, OR 97321, telephone (503) 929-5123, Jan Striplan, contact.

Pacific Bartlett Pear Growers, Inc., 813 S.W. Adler, Suite 601, Portland, OR 97205, telephone (503) 223-8139.
   Send for an information kit on pears, including recipes and an order form for a pear slicer ($2.00 as of this writing).

Portland Saturday Market, 108 W. Burnside, Portland, OR 97209, telephone (503) 222-6072, Judy Bowen, contact.

Salem Public Market, 1240 Rural Street, S.E., Salem, OR 97302, telephone (503) 393-0716, Rose Machalek, contact, or P.O. Box 3536, Salem, OR 97302, telephone (503) 362-6051, Natalie Rowe, contact.

Smith's Forest Fresh Products, Inc., 4716 N.E. 97th, Portland, OR 97220, telephone (503) 254-0164, Arly Smith, contact.

Weppler's Organically Grown Produce, 36000 Northern Drive, Brownsville, OR 97327, telephone (503) 466-3052, George H. Weppler, contact.

Pennsylvania

Reading Terminal Market, Twelfth and Arch Streets, Philadelphia, PA 19107, telephone (215) 922-2317, David K. O'Neil, general manager.

Seafood

Illinois

Carolyn Collins Caviar, P.O. Box 662, Crystal Lake, IL 60014, telephone (312) 226-0342, Bill Dugan or Rachel Collins, contact.

Maine

Ducktrap River Fish Farm, Inc., RFD 2, Box 378, Lincolnville, ME 04849, telephone (207) 763-3960.
   Send for a mail-order catalog of their line of smoked fish and shellfish.

Horton's Downeast Foods, Inc. Gristmill Road, P.O. Box 430, Waterboro, ME 04087, telephone (800) 346-6066 outside Maine, (207) 247-6900 in Maine, Don and Jean Horton, contacts.

Oregon

Green's Seafood, 6767 S.W. Macadam Avenue, Portland, OR 97219, telephone (503) 246-8245, Larry Gyure and Richard Marak, contacts.

RUSHING WATERS TROUT FARM, INC., N301 Highway H, P.O. Box 386, Palmyra, WI 53156, telephone (414) 495-2089, William D. Johnson, manager, Michael A. Ward, sales representative.

Meats, Poultry, and Game

CALIFORNIA

MARCEL & HENRI CHARCUTERIE FRANÇAISE, 415 Browning Way, South San Francisco, CA 94080, telephone (800) 227-6436 outside California, (800) 542-4230 in California, Henri Lapuyade, president.
    Send for mail-order catalog.

NIGHT BIRD GAME & POULTRY COMPANY, 650 San Mateo Avenue, San Bruno, CA 94066, telephone (415) 873-1940.

ILLINOIS

WILD GAME, INC., 2315 West Huron, Chicago, IL 60612, telephone (312) 278-1661, Kaye Zubow, president.
    Send for mail-order catalog.

NEW YORK

COMMONWEALTH ENTERPRISES, LTD., P.O. Box 49, Airport Road, Mongaup Valley, NY 12762, telephone (914) 583-6630, Howard Josephs, contact.
    Celebrated for their duck foie gras, the Josephs also carry a line of fresh whole duck, boneless breasts, legs, giblets, rendered duck fat, and smoked specialties. Send for catalog.

RHODE ISLAND

ANTONELLI POULTRY COMPANY, INC., 62 DePasquale Avenue, Providence, RI 02903, telephone (401) 621-9377, Chris Morris, proprietor.
    Supplies southern New England with fresh game, poultry, and eggs. A small operation but well worth the visit, during regular business hours, Monday through Friday.

Cheese and Dairy Products

CALIFORNIA

LAURA CHENEL'S CHÈVRE, 1550 Ridley Avenue, Santa Rosa, CA 95401, telephone (707) 575-8888, Laura Chenel, proprietor.
    One of the first producers of a domestic goat cheese. Send for catalog.

MARIN FRENCH CHEESE COMPANY, 7500 Red Hill Road, Petaluma, CA 94953, telephone (707) 762-6001, W. Douglas Johnstone, director of sales.
    Tours available every day from 10:00 A.M. through 4:00 P.M. Closed Thanksgiving, Christmas, and New Year's Day.

SONOMA CHEESE FACTORY, 2 Spain Street, Sonoma, CA 95476, telephone (707) 996-1000.
    Send for gift catalog.

VELLA CHEESE COMPANY, P.O. Box 191, Sonoma, CA 95476-0191, telephone (800) 848-0505 or (707) 938-3232, Ignazio Vella, proprietor.
    The gregarious owner, Ig Vella, who is responsible for one of the most unique cheeses in the United States, offers informal tours of his store and factory at 315 Second Street East, Sonoma. Write or telephone first. The store is open Monday through Saturday, from 9:00 A.M. to 6:00 P.M., and Sunday, from 10:00 A.M. to 5:00 P.M.

ILLINOIS

KOLB-LENA CHEESE COMPANY, 3990 North Sunnyside Road, Lena, IL 61048, telephone (815) 369-4577, Patrick J. Cardiff, manufacturing director.
    Makers of Delico Brand Brie, Camembert, feta, and baby Swiss. Because of Health Department regulations, tours are not offered. There is, however, a retail store at the plant, and a mail-order catalog is available upon request.

IOWA

MAYTAG DAIRY FARMS, INC., Box 806, Newton, IA 50208, telephone (800) 247-2458 outside Iowa, (800) 258-2437 in Iowa.
    Visitors are welcome Monday through Friday, from 8:00 A.M. to 5:00 P.M., and Saturday, from 9:00 A.M. to 1:00 P.M. Call for details and to order a cheese catalog.

MASSACHUSETTS

CRAIGSTON CHEESE COMPANY, 45 Dodges Row, Box 267, Wenham, MA 01984, telephone (508) 468-7497, Susan A. Hollander, contact.

NEW ENGLAND

THE AMERICAN CHEESE SOCIETY, P.O. Box 97, Ashfield, MA 01330.
    Send for "A Guide to American Specialty and Farmstead Cheeses" ($3.50 plus $1 shipping and handling).

PENNSYLVANIA

FLEUR DE LAIT FOODS, LTD., 254 South Custer Avenue, New Holland, PA 17557, telephone (717) 354-4411.
    Produces a fine line of soft, low-fat cheeses. Send for mail-order catalog and information.

VERMONT

CABOT FARMER'S COOPERATIVE CREAMERY, Box 128, Cabot, VT 05647, telephone (802) 563-2231, Ann M. Dixon, contact.

VERMONT DEPARTMENT OF AGRICULTURE, 116 State Street, Montpelier, VT 05602, telephone (802) 828-2212.
    Send for a complete list of cheese producers in the state of Vermont.

WISCONSIN

RYSER'S CHALET, 209 East Main Street, Mt. Horeb, WI 53572, telephone (608) 437-3051, Carla Werger, manager.

Products available by mail order from TASTE OF WISCONSIN, P.O. Box 6035, Ocala, FL 32678, telephone (904) 732-4415.

WISCONSIN MILK MARKETING BOARD, 8418 Excelsior Drive, Madison, WI 53711, telephone (800) 373-8820 or (608) 836-8820, Linda Funk, national communications manager.

Breweries

CALIFORNIA

ANCHOR BREWING COMPANY, 1705 Mariposa Street, San Francisco, CA 94107, telephone (415) 863-8350, Linda Rowe, contact.

Tours available by appointment, Monday through Friday. Please call at least one week in advance.

BIERS BRASSERIE, 33 East San Francisco Street, San Jose, CA 95113, telephone (408) 297-3766.

HEALDSBURG BREWING COMPANY & VINTNER'S GRILL, 347 Healdsburg Avenue, Healdsburg, CA 95448, telephone (707) 433-BEER.

SAN ANDREAS BREWING COMPANY, 737 San Benito Street, Hollister, CA 95023, telephone (408) 637-7074.

SEA CLIFF CAFÉ, 1801 Clement Street, San Francisco, CA 94118, telephone (415) 386-6266, Klaus Lange, proprietor.

Lange, a restaurateur, chef, furniture maker, artist, and marketing genius, is a restaurant legend in San Francisco. He brews an excellent beer, Dutch Brown Ale.

WILLETT'S BREWERY, 902 Main Street, Napa, CA 94558.

CONNECTICUT

THE CONNECTICUT BREWING COMPANY, P.O. Box 10751, Elmwood, CT 06110, telephone (203) 247-4752, John B. Foley, president.

Makers of Nathan Hale Golden Lager. Send for promotional material.

MASSACHUSETTS

THE BOSTON BEER COMPANY, 30 Germania Street, Boston, MA 02130, telephone (617) 522-3400, Richard J. Godwin, contact.

Makers of Samuel Adams Beer. The company can be reached by phone twenty-four hours a day. Write for tour information.

OREGON

THE BLITZ-WEINHARD BREWING COMPANY, 1133 West Burnside Street, Portland, OR 97209, telephone (503) 222-4351, Marsha Stout, tour coordinator.

BRIDGEPORT BREW PUB, 1313 N.W. Marshall, Portland, OR 97209, telephone (503) 241-7179, Nancy Ponzi, contact.

Open Tuesday through Thursday, from 4:00 to 10:00 P.M., Friday, from 4:00 to 11:00 P.M., and Sunday, from 1:00 to 8:00 P.M.

HILLSDALE BREWERY, 1505 S.W. Sunset Boulevard, Portland, OR 97201, telephone (503) 246-3938, Mike McMenamin, contact.

OREGON TRAIL BREWERY, 341 S.W. Second Street, Corvallis, OR 97333, telephone (503) 758-3527.

PORTLAND BREWING COMPANY, 1339 N.W. Flanders Street, Portland, OR 97209, telephone (503) 222-7150, Art Larrance, contact.
Open from 11:00 A.M. to 11:00 P.M., except Saturdays, when open until midnight.

JAMES WALSH BREWERY, 1840 Patterson, Eugene, OR 97405, telephone (503) 485-2294, James Walsh, contact.

WIDMER BREWING COMPANY, 1405 N.W. Lovejoy (corner of S.W. 9th and Salmon), Portland, OR 97209, telephone (503) 227-7276, Kurt or Rob Widmer, contact.

VERMONT

THE VERMONT PUB-BREWERY OF BURLINGTON, 114 College Street, Burlington, VT 05401, telephone (802) 865-0500.

Wineries and Distilleries

CALIFORNIA

BERINGER VINEYARDS, 2000 Main Street, St. Helena, Napa Valley, CA 94574, telephone (707) 963-7115.

CHATEAU SOUVERAIN'S WINE COUNTRY NEWS, Winenews, P.O. Box 528, Alexander Valley, Geyserville, CA 95441.
Copies available to subscribers free of charge.

FETZER VINEYARDS, 5040 Commercial Circle, Suite A, Concord, CA 94520, telephone (415) 680-7422, Sid Goldstein, food concepts director.

QUADY WINERY, P.O. Box 728, Madera, CA 93639, telephone (209) 673-8068.

SONOMA COUNTY WINERIES ASSOCIATION, Luther Burbank Center for the Arts, 50 Mark West Springs Road, Santa Rosa, CA 95403.

NEW ENGLAND

THE NEW ENGLAND WINE COUNCIL, Chicama Vineyard, Stony Hill Road, West Tisbury, MA 02575, George Mathiesen, president.
Write for information and brochures on the wineries and vineyards of New England.

OREGON

ADELSHEIM VINEYARDS, 22150 N. E. Quarter Mile Lane, Newberg, OR 97132-9159, David B. and Virginia Adelsheim, contacts.
The winery is open for two annual events *only:* "Rain Revels," on the

second weekend in June, and Thanksgiving weekend. Please write to be included on the mailing list.

AMITY VINEYARDS, 18150 Amity Vineyards Road, S.E., Amity, OR 97101-9603, telephone (503) 835-2362 for the vineyard, (503) 843-3787 for the tasting room, Myron Redford, president and winemaker, Vikki Wetle, director of public relations.

The tasting room is open daily from 11:30 A.M. to 5:30 P.M. Special events include the Summer Solstice Festival, held on the third weekend in June, the Pinot Noir Release, held on the third weekend in September, and the Harvest Party, usually held on the last weekend in October, but "the grapes schedule this one."

BETHEL HEIGHTS VINEYARD, 6060 Bethel Heights Road N.W., Salem, OR 97304, telephone (503) 581-2262.

New wine releases are featured at the Memorial Day Weekend Tastevin Tour, held on May 28 through 30, from 12:00 to 6:00 P.M. Regular tasting room hours, Tuesday through Sunday, from 11:00 A.M. to 5:00 P.M. Call or write for updated calendar before visiting.

CLEAR CREEK DISTILLERY, 1430 Northwest 23rd Avenue, Portland, OR 97210, telephone (503) 248-9470, Stephen R. McCarthy, proprietor.

EYRIE VINEYARDS, 935 East 10th Avenue, McMinnville, OR 97128, telephone (503) 472-6315 for the winery, (503) 864-2410 for the vineyard, David R. and Diana Lett, winemakers.

Annual Thanksgiving weekend winetasting. Private visits for small groups can be arranged throughout the year by appointment.

OREGON WINEGROWERS ASSOCIATION, P.O. Box 6590, Portland, OR 97228-6590, telephone (503) 233-2377.

Send for their "Discover Oregon Wineries" guide.

PONZI VINEYARDS, Route 1, Box 842, Beaverton, OR 97005, telephone (503) 628-1227, Richard and Nancy Ponzi, proprietors.

SALEM CONVENTION & VISITORS ASSOCIATION, 1313 Mill Street S.E., Salem, OR 97301, telephone (503) 581-4325.

Send for information on Salem area wineries.

RHODE ISLAND

SAKONNET VINEYARDS, P.O. Box 197, Little Compton, RI 02837, telephone (401) 635-8486, Joetta Kirk, vineyard manager.

Send for information on their Master Chef Educational Series.

Vinegar

CALIFORNIA

KIMBERLY VINEGAR WORKS, P.O. Box 40, Hunter's Point, San Francisco, CA 94124, telephone (415) 822-5850, Larry and Ruth Robinson, proprietors.

Fruits, Sweets, and Condiments

CALIFORNIA

CALIFORNIA OLIVE INDUSTRY, P.O. Box 4098, Fresno, CA 93744, telephone (209) 486-1383.
   Write for recipe ideas, specifying whether your interest is consumer or food service recipes.

THE CHERRY TREE COMPANY, INC., P.O. Box 361, Sonoma, CA 95476 (at highways 12 and 121), telephone (707) 938-3480.
   Send for a mail-order list.

GOLDEN GATE LTD., P.O. Box 1050, Windsor, CA 95492, telephone (707) 838-0223, Carol and Bill Adams, proprietors.
   Makers of an exceptional line of fine liqueur cakes. Send for a catalog.

MAINE

MOTHER'S MOUNTAIN MUSTARD, Tan-Man, 110 Woodville Road, Falmouth, ME 04105, telephone (207) 781-4658.
   Send for a mail-order catalog.

MARYLAND

CALVERT SPECIALTY FOOD PRODUCTS, 23 Dorchester Court, Annapolis, MD 21403, telephone (301) 268-3902, Rita Calvert, proprietor.
   Produces a line of unique mustards. Write for a catalog.

MASSACHUSETTS

HARBOR SWEETS, Palmer Cove, 85 Leavitt Street, Salem, MA 01970, telephone (800) 225-5669 for orders, (800) 234-4860 for customer service.
   Visitors are welcome to visit the chocolate factory. Hours from September through June are from 8:30 A.M. to 4:30 P.M., Monday through Friday, and Saturday, from 9:00 A.M. to 3:00 P.M. During July and August, hours are from 9:00 A.M. to 3:00 P.M., Monday through Saturday. Call or write for information and a mail-order catalog.

OREGON

OREGON DEPARTMENT OF AGRICULTURE, 121 S.W. Salmon Street, Suite 240, Portland, OR 97204-2987, telephone (503) 229-6734.
   For a list of the many unique specialty food items available by mail, write for a copy of "Oregon's Bounty."

VERMONT

BLANCHARD & BLANCHARD, LTD., P.O. Box 1080, Norwich, VT 05055, telephone (802) 649-1327.

BREAD & CHOCOLATE, 125 Bixby Hill Road, Essex Junction, VT 05452.
   Send for a catalog listing their chocolate sauces.

WOOD'S CIDER JELLY, RFD 2, Box 266, Springfield, VT 05156, telephone (802) 263-5547, Willis and Tina Wood, proprietors.
   Visitors are invited to observe jelly production from October until mid-December.

WISCONSIN

WISCONSIN WILDERNESS FOOD PRODUCTS, INC., 7841 North 47th Street, Milwaukee, WI 53223, telephone (414) 355-0001.
Send for their list of sauces, condiments, and dessert toppings.

Miscellaneous

IDAHO

AMERICAN DRY PEA & LENTIL ASSOCIATION, 5071 Highway 8 West, Moscow, ID 83843, telephone (208) 882-3023.
Send for recipes and nutritional information on legumes.

MASSACHUSETTS

CRANBERRY WORLD MUSEUM, 225 Water Street, Plymouth, MA 02360, telephone (508) 747-2350.
Visitors are welcome from April 1 through November 30, every day, from 9:30 A.M. to 5:00 P.M.

MINNESOTA

CHICAGO CUTLERY, 5420 North County Road 18, Minneapolis, MN 55428.
Send for "Knife Knowledge," their booklet on knife safety, handling, sharpening, and carving.

NEW YORK

SAN PELLEGRINO USA, Box 1367, New York, NY 10101-1367.
Send for the free booklet, "To Your Health."

INTERNATIONAL OLIVE OIL COUNCIL, J.A.F. Station, P.O. Box 2197, New York, NY 10116.
Send for the free booklet, "The Flavor of the Mediterranean."

OREGON

PORTLAND CULINARY ALLIANCE, 2775 S.W. Sherwood Drive, Portland, OR 97201, Laura Barton, contact.
This nonprofit group provides professional and educational opportunities for people in the food and wine community in Oregon. Request a membership application.

INDEX

If you would like one or more copies of *A Taste for All Seasons*, by the chefs of ARA Fine Dining in association with David Paul Larousse, please write to

The Harvard Common Press
535 Albany Street
Boston, Massachusetts 02118

A Taste for All Seasons is available in hardcover for $24.95. When ordering, please enclose a check or money order for the full price plus $3.00 for postage and handling. If you are a Massachusetts resident, please add 5 percent sales tax.

The Harvard Common Press also publishes several other cookbooks. We would be happy to send you our catalogue at no charge. Just write us at the above address.